Lalita Tripura Sundari Shodashi Tantra Mahavidya

A book of Forbidden knowledge

Daniella Christoff
Ramesh Chaturvedi

DARKTEXT PUBLISHERS

First Published in **July 2026**

ISBN: 978-93-6356-163-2

DARKTEXT PUBLISHERS

+91 9311101365

Distributed by: Watergies

Preface

There is magic. Most would believe that it is extinct, that it might have been, but it is lost through history. That is what the guidance intended on in the first place, it had to be esoteric. It is not extinct, but just endangered, and it will forever be, because divinity will always stay in its place, it is just the worshipper who comes and goes, and those who find it, might reap the fruits of their practice.

Foreword

The authors take you on a remarkable journey as you explore the Puranic tantra, the third of its kind, the greatest Mahavidya - the Lalita Tripura Sundari Shodashi Tantra. Scary, overwhelming, testing, but accomplishing, indulging and fruitful, this is the theme of this Tantra, and I have never seen a clearer take, for any common person to understand it better. This is what magic is all about.

Acknowledgments

A special thanks to the publishing team for everything you have done for us, for letting us bring years of research to light, that can be understood by anyone and everyone who wants to accomplish their desires.

About the authors

Daniella Christoff and Ramesh Chaturvedi found themselves researching the Mahavidyas, in a corner of the world not many know about. Their passion for discovering and unlocking the powerful secrets of divinity and the universe put them together on compiling the Mahavidyas, like they understood it. Their research starts here, and opens up anyone to understand it in the simplest way ever that existed, while they go deeper and deeper in their expedition to experience and present to the world all powers that exist, and how to tap them. They intend on getting there someday soon.

Dedication

This book is dedicated to the devotees and practitioners who not only practice the magic and the art to perfection, but are more than happy to introduce you to the depth of the practice, if you just take the initiative to find them. They are there in plain sight, if you only know their history and where to find them. The things that they showed us and the connections that we made can only be magic, and nothing else.

Introduction

Some call it a Mahavidya - the greatest knowledge, and there are just ten of those, with this the third one, while others would call it forbidden knowledge, because it is that powerful as it changes one's perspective of reality. Most would not believe it still exists, but in the corners of the world that no one wants you to know about, practitioners achieve everything that they ever wanted, and such is the power of the Lalita Tripura Sundari Shodashi Tantra. It is pure magic, and this conversation between the Gods - Shiva and Parvati in their Bhairava and Bhairavi form detail every single bit of the practice. This book has kept it pronounceable according to the origin, and explained it to make it understandable for those indulged in the practice, and even for those who are just dabbling to explore it.

Prologue

'The wise practitioner who recites it one thousand times daily for half a month will surely find the entire world brought into submission, as though it had become his servant.

A person who daily offers oblations with Palash flowers while reciting each name gains influence over all maidens dwelling on Earth, as well as those abiding in other worlds.'

Note : You should be familiar with Kali Tantra and Tara Tantra before getting into this, and in comparison, the rituals and the results coming from this are much simpler to follow. Divine magic is accessible, but it should be dealt with caution. Do not misuse it in any way, since you never know if what goes around, comes back around.

Contents

Preface

Foreword

Acknowledgement

About the Author

Dedication

Introduction

Prologue

Chapter One - Puja Patala - The Chapter of Worship 1

Chapter Two - Nyasa Patala - The Chapter of Consecration 10

Chapter Three - Mala Patala - The Chapter of Garland 21

Chapter Four - Phala Patala - The Chapter of benefits 40

Chapter Five - Srividya Patala - The Chapter of Revelation 84

Chapter Six - Stotram Patala - The Chapter of Litany 102

Epilogue

ॐ ऐं ह्रीं श्रीं त्रिपुर सुंदरीयै नमः

Om Aim Hreem Shreem
Tripura Sundariyai Namah

Chapter One

Puja Patala

The Chapter of Worship

कैलासशिखरासीनं देवदेवं जगद्गुरुम् ।

पप्रच्छेशं परानन्दं भैरवी परमेश्वरम् ॥ १॥

Pronunciation

kailāsaśikharāsīnaṃ devadevaṃ jagadgurum ।

papraccheśaṃ parānandaṃ bhairavī parameśvaram ॥ 1 ॥

Meaning

On the pristine peaks of Mount Kailash, Goddess Parvati in Bhairavi form addresses Shiva, the god of gods in Bhairava form.

श्रीभैरव्युवाच ।

कौलेश श्रोतुमिच्छामि सर्वमन्त्रोत्तमोत्तमम् ।

ललिताया शतनाम सर्वकामफलप्रदम् ॥ २॥

Pronunciation

śrībhairavyuvāca ।

kauleśa śrotumicchāmi
sarvamantrōttamottamam ।

Lalitayāḥ śatanāma
sarvakāmaphalapradam ॥ 2 ॥

Meaning

Bhairav says, Oh Lord of the Kaulas, I desire to hear the hundred names of Lalita, that is supreme among all mantras and fulfils every desire.

श्रीभैरवोवाच ।

शृणु देवि महाभागे स्तोत्रमेतदनुत्तमम् ।

पठनाद्धारणादस्य सर्वसिद्धीश्वरो भवेत् ॥३॥

Pronunciation

śrībhairavovāca ।

śṛṇu devi mahābhāge
stotrametadanuttamam ।

paṭhanāddhāraṇādasya
sarvasiddhīśvaro bhavet ॥ 3 ॥

Meaning

Bhairava says, Oh great fortunate Goddess, reciting this unsurpassed hymn, or just knowing it in memory, one becomes a lord among those possessed of all siddhis.

षट्कर्माणि च सिद्ध्यन्ति स्तवस्यास्य प्रसादतः ।

गोपनीयं पशोरग्रे स्वयोनिमपरे यथा ॥ ४॥

Pronunciation

ṣaṭkarmāṇi ca siddhyanti
stavasyāsya prasādataḥ ।

gopanīyaṃ paśoragre
svayonimapare yathā ॥ 4 ॥

Meaning

By the grace of this hymn, these six tantric rites are accomplished. It must be kept secret from the uninitiated, just as a woman carefully guards one's own yoni.

ललिताया लकारादि नामशतकस्य देवि ।

राजराजेश्वरो ऋषिः प्रोक्तो छन्दोऽनुष्टुप् तथा ॥ ५॥

Pronunciation

Lalitayā lakārādi nāmaśatakasya devi ।

rājarājeśvaro ṛṣiḥ prokto chando'nuṣṭup tathā ॥ 5 ॥

Meaning

Oh Goddess, for these hundred names of Lalita beginning with the letter La, the seer (rsi) is said to be Rajarajesvara, and the metre is Anustubh.

देवता ललितादेवी षट्कर्मसिद्ध्यर्थे तथा ।
धर्मार्थकाममोक्षेषु विनियोगः प्रकीर्तितः ॥ ६॥

Pronunciation

devatā Lalitadevī
ṣaṭkarmasiddhyarthe tathā ।

dharmārthakāmamokṣeṣu
viniyogaḥ prakīrtitaḥ ॥ 6 ॥

Meaning

The presiding deity is Goddess Lalita and its application is prescribed for the accomplishment of the six rites and for the attainment of Dharma, Artha, Kāma, and Moksha.

वाक्-काम-शक्तिबीजेन करषडङ्गमाचरेत् ।

प्रयोगे बालात्र्यक्षरी योजयित्वा जपं चरेत् ॥ ७॥

Pronunciation

vāk-kāma-śaktibījena karaṣaḍaṅgamācaret ।

prayoge bālātryakṣarī yojayitvā japaṃ caret ॥ 7 ॥

Meaning

One should perform the sixfold hand nyasa using the seed syllables of speech, desire and power. In ritual application, one should unite it with the three syllabled Bala mantra and then recite it.

इति प्रथमः पटलः ॥

iti prathamaḥ paṭalaḥ ॥

This ends the First Chapter, the Puja Patala or Chapter of Worship, in the Lalita Tripura Sundari Shodashi Tantra.

Chapter Two

Nyasa Patala

The Chapter of Consecration

करन्यासः

Kara-nyāsa

ओं ऐं अङ्गुष्ठाभ्यां नमः ।

ओं क्लीं तर्जनीभ्यां नमः ।

ओं सौः मध्यमाभ्यां नमः ।

ओं ऐं अनामिकाभ्यां नमः ।

ओं क्लीं कनिष्ठिकाभ्यां नमः ।

ओं सौः करतलकरपृष्ठाभ्यां नमः ।

Pronunciation

oṃ aiṃ aṅguṣṭhābhyāṃ namaḥ ।

oṃ klīṃ tarjanībhyāṃ namaḥ ।

oṃ sauḥ madhyamābhyāṃ namaḥ ।

oṃ aiṃ anāmikābhyāṃ namaḥ ।

oṃ klīṃ kaniṣṭhikābhyāṃ namaḥ ।

oṃ sauḥ karatalakarapṛṣṭhābhyāṃ namaḥ ।

Meaning

One should install the sacred syllables upon the hands:

Om Aim – obeisance to the thumbs.

Om Klim – obeisance to the index fingers.

Om Sauh – obeisance to the middle fingers.

Om Aim – obeisance to the ring fingers.

Om Klim – obeisance to the little fingers.

Om Sauh – obeisance to the palms and backs of the hands.

अङ्गन्यासः

Aṅga-nyāsa

ओं ऐं हृदयाय नमः ।

ओं क्लीं शिरसे स्वाहा ।

ओं सौः शिखायै वषट् ।

ओं ऐं कवचाय हुम् ।

ओं क्लीं नेत्रत्रयाय वौषट् ।

ओं सौः अस्त्राय फट् ।

Pronunciation

om̐ aiṃ hṛdayāya namaḥ ।

oṃ klīṃ śirase svāhā ।

oṃ sauḥ śikhāyai vaṣaṭ ।

oṃ aiṃ kavacāya huṃ ।

oṃ klīṃ netratrayāya vauṣaṭ ।

oṃ sauḥ astrāya phaṭ ।

Meaning

One should install the sacred syllables upon the body:

* Om Aim – obeisance to the heart.

* Om Klīm – svaha to the head.

* Om Sauh – vasat to the crown-lock.

* Om Aiṃ – hum to the protective armour.

* Om Klim – vausat to the three eyes.

* Om Sauh – phat to the missile-weapon.

अथ ध्यानम्

Dhyāna

बालार्कमण्डलाभासां चतुर्बाहुं त्रिलोचनाम् ।
पाशाङ्कुशधनुर्बाणान् धारयन्तीं शिवां भजे ॥

Pronunciation

bālārkamaṇḍalābhāsāṃ
caturbāhuṃ trilocanām ।

pāśāṅkuśadhanurbāṇān
dhārayantīṃ śivāṃ bhaje ॥

Meaning

I adore the auspicious Goddess, radiant like the orb of the rising sun, three eyed and four armed, bearing the noose, goad, bow and arrows.

इति द्वितीयः पटलः ॥

iti dvitīyaḥ paṭalaḥ ||

This ends the Second Chapter, the Nyasa Patala or Chapter of Consecration, in the Lalita Tripura Sundari Shodashi Tantra.

Chapter Three

Mala Patala

The Chapter of Garland

ललिता लक्ष्मी लोलाक्षी लक्ष्मणा लक्ष्मणार्चिता ।

लक्ष्मणप्राणरक्षिणी लाकिनी लक्ष्मणप्रिया ॥ १॥

Pronunciation

Lalita lakṣmī lolākṣī lakṣmaṇā lakṣmaṇārcitā ।

lakṣmaṇaprāṇarakṣiṇī lākinī lakṣmaṇapriyā ॥ 1 ॥

Meaning

She is Lalita, Lakshmi, the Lovely Eyed One, the Auspicious Lady, worshipped by the virtuous, the Protectress of life, Lakini and the Beloved of those endowed with auspicious marks.

लोला लकारा लोमेशा लोलजिह्वा लज्जावती ।

लक्ष्या लाक्ष्या लक्षरता लकाराक्षरभूषिता ॥ २॥

Pronunciation

lolā lakārā lomeśā lolajihvā lajjāvatī
।

lakṣyā lākṣyā lakṣaratā
lakārākṣarabhūṣitā ॥ 2 ॥

Meaning

She is Playful, the Embodiment of the Letter La, Mistress of the Body, Restless Tongued, and Modest, the Goal, the Marked One, Delighting in the Aim and Adorned with the syllable La.

लोललयात्मिका लीला लीलावती च लाङ्गली ।

लावण्यामृतसारा च लावण्यामृतदीर्घिका ॥ ३॥

Pronunciation

lolalayātmikā līlā līlāvatī ca lāṅgalī ।

lāvaṇyāmṛtasārā ca
lāvaṇyāmṛtadīrghikā ॥ 3 ॥

Meaning

She is the Essence of Playful Dissolution, Divine Play itself, the Playful One, and the Bearer of the Plough, the Essence of the Nectar of Beauty and the Vast Reservoir of that Nectar.

लज्जा लज्जामती लज्जा ललना ललनप्रिया ।
लवणा लवली लसा लाक्षकी लुब्धा लालसा ॥
४॥

Pronunciation

lajjā lajjāmatī lajjā lalanā lalanapriyā ।

lavaṇā lavalī lasā lākṣakī lubdhā lālasā ॥ 4 ॥

Meaning

She is Modesty, Possessed of Modesty, the Bashful One, the Maiden, and Lover of Maidens, Graceful, Charming, Radiant, Lac-Dyed, Passionate and Filled with Longing.

लोकमाता लोकपूज्या लोकजननी लोलुपा ।

लोहिता लोहिताक्षी च लिङ्गाख्या चैव लिङ्गेशी ॥ ५॥

Pronunciation

lokamātā lokapūjyā lokajananī lolupā ।

lohitā lohitākṣī ca liṅgākhyā caiva liṅgeśī ॥ 5 ॥

Meaning

She is the Mother of the World, Worshipped by the World, the Creatrix of the World, and the Ever Eager One, the Red Goddess, Red Eyed, Known as the Linga and Mistress of the Linga.

लिङ्गगीति लिङ्गभवा लिङ्गमाला लिङ्गप्रिया ।

लिङ्गाभिधायिनी लिङ्गा लिङ्गनामसदानन्दा ॥ ६॥

Pronunciation

Lingagīti Lingabhavā Lingamālā
Lingapriyā ।

liṅgābhidhāyinī liṅgā
Linganāmasadānandā ॥ 6 ॥

Meaning

She is the Song of the Linga, Born of the Linga, Garlanded with the Linga, and Fond of the Linga, she is who Reveals the Linga, the Linga itself and Ever Blissful through the Name of the Linga.

लिङ्गामृतप्रीता लिङ्गार्चनप्रीता लिङ्गपूज्या ।

लिङ्गरूपा लिङ्गस्था च लिङ्गालिङ्गनतत्परा ॥ ७॥

Pronunciation

liṅgāmṛtaprītā liṅgārcanaprītā Lingapūjyā ।

Lingarūpā Lingasthā ca liṅgāLinganatatparā ॥ 7 ॥

Meaning

She delights in the nectar of the Linga, rejoices in the worship of the Linga, and is herself worthy of such worship, she is of the form of the Linga, abiding in the Linga and devoted to union with the Linga.

लतापूजनरता च लतासाधकतुष्टिदा ।

लतापूजकरक्षिणी लतासाधनसिद्धिदा ॥ ८॥

Pronunciation

Latapūjanaratā ca
Latasādhakatuṣṭidā ।

Latapūjakarakṣiṇī
Latasādhanasiddhidā ॥ 8 ॥

Meaning

She delights in the worship of the Lata, grants satisfaction to practitioners of the Lata rite, protects those who worship the Lata and bestows success in Lata sadhana.

लतागृहनिवासिनी लतापूज्या लताराध्या ।

लतापुष्पा लतारता लताधारा लतामयी ॥ ९॥

Pronunciation

Latagṛhanivāsinī Latapūjyā
Latarādhyā ।

Latapuṣpā Latāratā Latadhārā
Latamayī ॥ 9 ॥

Meaning

She dwells within the House of the Lata, is worshipped as the Lata, adored through the Lata, flower like as the Lata, delighting in the Lata, supporting the Lata and pervading it completely.

लतास्पर्शनसन्तुष्टा लताऽऽलिङ्गनहर्षिता ।

लताविद्या लतासारा लताऽऽचारा लतानिधी ॥

१०॥

Pronunciation

Latasparśanasantuṣṭā
LataLinganaharṣitā ।

Latavidyā Latasārā Latacārā
Latanidhī ॥ 10 ॥

Meaning

She is pleased by the touch of the Lata, delighted by its embrace, the Knowledge of the Lata, its Essence, its Sacred Practice and the Treasure of all that pertains to the Lata.

लवङ्गपुष्पसन्तुष्टा लवङ्गलतामध्यस्था ।

लवङ्गलतिकारूपा लवङ्गहोमसन्तुष्टा ॥ ११॥

Pronunciation

lavaṅgapuṣpasantuṣṭā
lavaṅgaLatamadhyasthā ।

lavaṅgalatikārūpā
lavaṅgahomasantuṣṭā ॥ 11 ॥

Meaning

She is pleased by offerings of clove flowers, abides amidst the clove creeper, assumes the form of the clove-vine, and is delighted by oblations offered with cloves in the sacred fire.

लकाराक्षारपूजिता च लकारवर्णोद्भवा ।

लकारवर्णभूषिता लकारवर्णरुचिरा ॥ १२॥

Pronunciation

lakārākṣārapūjitā ca
lakāravarṇodbhavā ।

lakāravarṇabhūṣitā
lakāravarṇarucirā ॥ 12 ॥

Meaning

She is worshipped through the sacred syllable La, born from the letter La, adorned with the letter La and is made beautiful by the splendour of that letter.

लकारबीजोद्भवा तथा लकाराक्षरस्थिता ।

लकारबीजनिलया लकारबीजसर्वस्वा ॥ १३॥

Pronunciation

lakārabījodbhavā tathā lakārākṣarasthitā ।

lakārabījanilayā lakārabījasarvasvā ॥ 13 ॥

Meaning

She arises from the seed of the letter La, abides within that sacred syllable, dwells in the La bija and is the very essence and totality of that seed mantra.

लकारवर्णसर्वाङ्गी लक्ष्यछेदनतत्परा ।

लक्ष्यधरा लक्ष्यघूर्णा लक्षजापेनसिद्धिदा ॥ १४॥

Pronunciation

lakāravarṇasarvāṅgī
lakṣyachedanatatparā ।

lakṣyadharā lakṣyaghūrṇā
lakṣajāpenasiddhidā ॥ 14 ॥

Meaning

Her entire form is composed of the letter La, she is intent upon striking the mark, bears the object of concentration, moves within the field of perception and grants accomplishment through one hundred thousand repetitions.

लक्षकोटिरूपधरा लक्षलीलाकलालया ।

लोकपालेनार्चिता च लाक्षारागविलेपना ॥ १५॥

Pronunciation

lakṣakoṭirūpadharā
lakṣalīlākalālayā ।

lokapālenārcitā ca
lākṣārāgavilepanā ॥ 15 ॥

Meaning

She assumes ten million forms, is the abode of countless divine plays and arts, is worshipped by the guardians of the worlds and is adorned with the crimson hue of the lac dye.

लोकातीता लोपामुद्रा लज्जाबीजस्वरूपिणी ।

लज्जाहीना लज्जामयी लोकयात्राविधायिनी ॥

१६॥

Pronunciation

lokātītā lopāmudrā
lajjābījasvarūpiṇī ।

lajjāhīnā lajjāmayī
lokayātrāvidhāyinī ॥ 16 ॥

Meaning

She transcends the worlds, is Lopamudra, embodies the seed of shyness, is beyond shame and yet filled with modesty and directs the course of worldly existence.

लास्यप्रिया लयकरी लोकलया लम्बोदरी ।
लघिमादिसिद्धिदात्री लावण्यनिधिदायिनी ।
लकारवर्णग्रथिता लम्बीजा ललिताम्बिका ॥ १७॥

Pronunciation

lāsyapriyā layakarī lokalayā lambodarī ।
laghimādisiddhidātrī lāvaṇyanidhidāyinī ।
lakāravarṇagrathitā lambījā Lalitambikā ॥ 17 ॥

Meaning

She delights in the graceful dance, brings about dissolution, absorbs the worlds into herself, and is the Vast Bellied One. She bestows the yogic powers beginning with laghima, grants the treasure of beauty, is woven from the letter La, arises from the La bija, and is Lalita Ambika herself.

इति तृतीयः पटलः ॥

iti tṛtīyaḥ paṭalaḥ ॥

This ends the Third Chapter, the Mala Patala or Chapter of Garland, in the Lalita Tripura Sundari Shodashi Tantra.

Chapter Four

Phala Patala

The Chapter of Benefits

इति ते कथितं देवि गुह्याद्गुह्यतरं परम् ।
प्रातःकाले च मध्याह्ने सायाह्ने च सदा निशि ।
यः पठेत् साधकश्रेष्ठो त्रैलोक्यविजयी भवेत् ॥ १ ॥

Pronunciation

iti te kathitaṃ devi
guhyādguhyataraṃ param ।

prātaḥkāle ca madhyāhne sāyāhne
ca sadā niśi ।

yaḥ paṭhet sādhakaśreṣṭho
trailokyavijayī bhavet ॥ 1 ॥

Meaning

Oh Goddess, this supreme secret, the secret of secrets been revealed to you. The foremost of practitioners who recites it at dawn, at midday, at dusk and during the night becomes victorious throughout the three worlds.

सर्वपापविनिर्मुक्तः स याति ललितापदम् ।

शून्यागारे शिवारण्ये शिवदेवालये तथा ॥ २ ॥

Pronunciation

sarvapāpavinirmuktaḥ sa yāti Lalitapadam ।

śūnyāgāre śivāraṇye śivadevālaye tathā ॥ 2 ॥

Meaning

Freed from all sins, he attains the state of Lalita. This hymn may be recited in a deserted dwelling, in a sacred forest of Shiva, or in a temple dedicated to Shiva.

शून्यदेशे तडागे च नदीतीरे चतुष्पथे ।

एकलिङ्गे ऋतुस्नातागेहे वेश्यागृहे तथा ॥ ३ ॥

Pronunciation

śūnyadeśe taḍāge ca nadītīre catuṣpathe ।

ekaliṅge ṛtusnātāgehe veśyāgṛhe tathā ॥ 3 ॥

Meaning

It can also be recited in a solitary place, beside a pond, on the bank of a river, at a crossroads, before a solitary Linga, in the house of a woman after her ritual bath or even in the house of a courtesan.

पठेदष्टोत्तरशतनामानि सर्वसिद्धये ।

साधको वाञ्छां यत्कुर्यात् तत्तथैव भविष्यति ॥ ४ ॥

Pronunciation

paṭhed aṣṭottaraśatanāmāni sarvasiddhaye ।

sādhako vāñchāṃ yat kuryāt tat tathaiva bhaviṣyati ॥ 4 ॥

Meaning

One should recite these one hundred and eight names for the attainment of all siddhis and whatever the practitioner desires, it will come true.

ब्रह्माण्डगोलके याश्च याः काश्चिज्जगतीतले ।

समस्ताः सिद्धयो देवि करामलकवत्सदा ॥ ५ ॥

Pronunciation

brahmāṇḍagolake yāśca yāḥ kāścij jagatītale ।

samastāḥ siddhayo devi karāmalakavat sadā ॥ 5 ॥

Meaning

Oh Goddess, all the siddhis that exist within the cosmic sphere and throughout the worlds become as readily accessible as an amalaka fruit resting in the palm of one's hand.

साधकस्मृतिमात्रेण यावन्त्यः सन्ति सिद्धयः ।

स्वयमायान्ति पुरतो जपादीनां तु का कथा ॥ ६ ॥

Pronunciation

sādhakasmṛtimātreṇa yāvantyaḥ santi siddhayaḥ ।

svayam āyānti purato japādīnāṃ tu kā kathā ॥ 6 ॥

Meaning

By merely remembering the practitioner, all siddhis draw near of their own accord. Then what is the need of the fruits gained through recitation and other practices ?

अयुतावर्तनाद्देवि पुरश्चर्याऽस्य गीयते ।

पुरश्चर्यायुतः स्तोत्रः सर्वकर्मफलप्रदः ॥ ७ ॥

Pronunciation

ayutāvartanād devi puraścaryāsya gīyate ।

puraścaryāyutaḥ stotraḥ sarvakarmaphalapradaḥ ॥ 7 ॥

Meaning

Oh Goddess, ten thousand repetitions are prescribed as the purascaraṇa of this hymn. When accompanied by such a purascarana, the stotram bestows the fruits of every rite and undertaking.

सहस्त्रं च पठेद्यस्तु मासार्धं साधकोत्तमः ।

दासीभूतं जगत्सर्वं मासार्धाद्भवति ध्रुवम् ॥ ८ ॥

Pronunciation

sahasraṃ ca paṭhed yastu
māsārdhaṃ sādhakottamaḥ ।

dāsībhūtaṃ jagatsarvaṃ māsārdhād
bhavati dhruvam ॥ 8 ॥

Meaning

The wise practitioner who recites it one thousand times daily for half a month will surely find the entire world brought into submission, as though it had become his servant.

नित्यं प्रतिनाम्ना हुत्वा पलाशकुसुमैर्नरः ।
भूलोकस्थाः सर्वकन्याः सर्वलोकस्थितास्तथा ॥ ९ ॥

Pronunciation

nityaṃ pratināmnā hutvā
palāśakusumair naraḥ ।

bhūlokasthāḥ sarvakanyāḥ
sarvalokasthitās tathā ॥ 9 ॥

Meaning

A person who daily offers oblations with Palash flowers while reciting each name gains influence over all maidens dwelling on Earth, as well as those abiding in other worlds.

पातालस्थाः सर्वकन्याः नागकन्याः यक्षकन्याः ।

वशीकुर्यान्मण्डलार्धात्संशयो नात्र विद्यते ॥ १० ॥

Pronunciation

pātālasthāḥ sarvakanyāḥ
nāgakanyāḥ yakṣakanyāḥ ।

vaśīkuryān maṇḍalārdhāt saṃśayo
nātra vidyate ॥ 10 ॥

Meaning

Within half a ritual cycle (mandala), he brings under his influence all maidens of the netherworld, the daughters of the Nagas, and the daughters of the Yaksas, without doubt.

अश्वत्थमूले पठेत् शतवारं ध्यानपूर्वकम् ।

तत् क्षणाद्व्याधिनाशश्च भवेद्देवि न संशयः ॥ ११ ॥

Pronunciation

aśvatthamūle paṭhet śatavāraṃ dhyānapūrvakam ।

tatkṣaṇād vyādhināśaś ca bhaved devi na saṃśayaḥ ॥ 11 ॥

Meaning

One who recites this hymn one hundred times beneath an Ashvattha tree, preceded by meditation, becomes freed from all diseases instantly, without any doubt.

शून्यागारे पठेत् स्तोत्रं सहस्त्रं ध्यानपूर्वकम् ।
लक्ष्मी प्रसीदति ध्रुवं स त्रैलोक्यं वशिष्यति ॥ १२ ॥

Pronunciation

śūnyāgāre paṭhet stotraṃ sahasraṃ dhyānapūrvakam ।

lakṣmī prasīdati dhruvaṃ sa trailokyaṃ vaśiṣyati ॥ 12 ॥

Meaning

One who recites the hymn a thousand times in a secluded place, preceded by meditation, certainly gains the favour of Lakshmi and comes to exercise dominion over the three worlds.

प्रेतवस्त्रं भौमे ग्राह्यं रिपुनाम च वेष्टितम् ।

प्राणप्रतिष्ठां कृत्वा तु पूजां चैव हि कारयेत् ॥ १३ ॥

Pronunciation

pretavastraṃ bhaume grāhyaṃ
ripunāma ca veṣṭitam ।

prāṇapratiṣṭhāṃ kṛtvā tu pūjāṃ
caiva hi kārayet ॥ 13 ॥

Meaning

On a Tuesday, one should obtain a cloth from a corpse, inscribe or wrap it with the name of the enemy, and perform the rite of prana pratistha, and then carry out its worship.

श्मशाने निखनेद्रात्रौ द्विसहस्रं पठेत्ततः ।

जिह्वास्तम्भनमाप्नोति सद्यो मूकत्वमाप्नुयात् ॥ १४ ॥

Pronunciation

śmaśāne nikhaned rātrau
dvisahasraṃ paṭhet tataḥ ।

jihvāstambhanam āpnoti sadyo
mūkatvam āpnuyāt ॥ 14 ॥

Meaning

Having buried it in the cremation ground at night, one should then recite the hymn two thousand times. Thereby one attains the power of arresting the tongue, and the intended target immediately becomes speechless.

श्मशाने च पठेत् स्तोत्रं अयुतार्धं सुबुद्धिमान् ।

शत्रुक्षयो भवेत् सद्यो नान्यथा मम भाषितम् ॥ १५ ॥

Pronunciation

śmaśāne ca paṭhet stotraṃ
ayutārdhaṃ subuddhimān ।

śatrukṣayo bhavet sadyo nānyathā
mama bhāṣitam ॥ 15 ॥

Meaning

A wise practitioner who recites the hymn five thousand times in the cremation ground brings about the immediate destruction of enemies, without any failure.

प्रेतवस्त्रं शनौ ग्राह्यं प्रतिनाम्ना सम्पुटितम् ।
शत्रुनाम लिखित्वा च प्राणप्रतिष्ठां कारयेत् ॥ १६ ॥

Pronunciation

pretavastraṃ śanau grāhyaṃ pratināmnā saṃpuṭitam ।

śatrunāma likhitvā ca prāṇapratiṣṭhāṃ kārayet ॥ 16 ॥

Meaning

On a Saturday, one should obtain a corpse cloth, enclose it with the recitation of each name, inscribe the enemy's name upon it, and perform the rite of pran pratistha.

ततः ललितां सम्पूज्य कृष्णधत्तूरपुष्पकैः ।

श्मशाने निखनेद्रात्रौ शतवारं पठेत् स्तोत्रम् ॥ १७ ॥

Pronunciation

tataḥ Lalitaṃ sampūjya
kṛṣṇadhattūrapuṣpakaiḥ ।

śmaśāne nikhaned rātrau
śatavāraṃ paṭhet stotram ॥ 17 ॥

Meaning

Then, having worshipped Lalita with black Datura flowers, one should bury it in the cremation ground at night and recite the hymn one hundred times.

ततो मृत्युमवाप्नोति देवराजसमोऽपि सः ।

श्मशानाङ्गारमादाय मङ्गले शनिवारे वा ॥ १८ ॥

Pronunciation

tato mṛtyum avāpnoti
devarājasamo'pi saḥ ।

śmaśānāṅgāram ādāya maṅgale
śanivāre vā ॥ 18 ॥

Meaning

Thereby even one who is equal in power to the king of the Gods meets with death. Alternatively, one may take charcoal from the cremation ground on a Tuesday or a Saturday ..

प्रेतवस्त्रेण संवेष्ट्य बध्नीयात् प्रेतरज्जुना ।

दशाभिमन्त्रितं कृत्वा खनेद्वैरिवेश्मनि ॥ १९ ॥

Pronunciation

pretavastreṇa saṃveṣṭya badhnīyāt pretarajjunā ।

daśābhimantritaṃ kṛtvā khaned vairiveśmani ॥ 19 ॥

Meaning

Wrapping it in a corpse cloth and binding it with a funerary cord, one should empower it with ten recitations of the mantra and bury it in the enemy's dwelling.

सप्तरात्रान्तरे तस्योच्चाटनं भ्रामणं भवेत् ।

कुमारीं पूजयित्वा तु यः पठेद्भक्तितत्परः ॥ २० ॥

Pronunciation

saptarātrāntare tasyoccāṭanaṃ bhrāmaṇaṃ bhavet ।

kumārīṃ pūjayitvā tu yaḥ paṭhed bhaktitatparaḥ ॥ 20 ॥

Meaning

Within seven nights, the enemy is driven away and expelled. But one who, devoted to the Goddess, worships a maiden (kumari) and then recites the hymn...

न किञ्चिद्दुर्लभं तस्य दिवि वा भुवि मोदते ।

दुर्भिक्षे राजपीडायां सङ्ग्रामे वैरिमध्यके ॥ २१ ॥

Pronunciation

na kiñcid durlabhaṃ tasya divi vā bhuvi modate ।

durbhikṣe rājapīḍāyāṃ saṅgrāme vairimadhyake ॥ 21 ॥

Meaning

Nothing is difficult for him to obtain, whether in heaven or on Earth. In times of famine, royal oppression, warfare or when surrounded by enemies, he remains protected and prospers.

यत्र यत्र भयं प्राप्तः सर्वत्र प्रपठेन्नरः ।

तत्र तत्राभयं तस्य भवत्येव न संशयः ॥ २२ ॥

Pronunciation

yatra yatra bhayaṃ prāptaḥ
sarvatra prapaṭhen naraḥ ।

tatra tatrābhayaṃ tasya bhavatyeva
na saṃśayaḥ ॥ 22 ॥

Meaning

Whenever and wherever fear arises, one should recite this hymn. In every such situation, he will become fearless without any doubt.

वामपार्श्वे समानीय शोधितां वरकामिनीम् ।

जपं कृत्वा पठेद्यस्तु तस्य सिद्धिः करे स्थिता ॥ २३ ॥

Pronunciation

vāmapārśve samānīya śodhitāṃ varakāminīm ।

japaṃ kṛtvā paṭhed yastu tasya siddhiḥ kare sthitā ॥ 23 ॥

Meaning

Having seated a duly purified and worthy woman at his left side, one who performs the prescribed recitation and then recites this hymn finds accomplishment resting in the palm of his hand.

दरिद्रस्तु चतुर्दश्यां कामिनीसङ्गमैः सह ।

अष्टवारं पठेद्यस्तु कुबेरसदृशो भवेत् ॥ २४ ॥

Pronunciation

daridras tu caturdaśyāṃ
kāminīsaṅgamaiḥ saha ।

aṣṭavāraṃ paṭhed yastu
kuberasadṛśo bhavet ॥ 24 ॥

Meaning

A poor man who, on the fourteenth lunar day (chaturdashi), recites this hymn eight times in conjunction with the union with his consort becomes equal to Kubera in wealth.

श्रीललितां महादेवी नित्यं सम्पूज्य मानवः ।

प्रतिनाम्ना जुहुयात्स धनराशिमवाप्नुयात् ॥ २५ ॥

Pronunciation

śrīLalitaṃ mahādevī nityaṃ
sampūjya mānavaḥ ।

pratināmnā juhuyāt sa dhanarāśim
avāpnuyāt ॥ 25 ॥

Meaning

A person who daily worships Lalita Mahadevi and offers oblations with each of her names obtains an abundance of wealth.

नवनीतं चाभिमन्त्र्य स्त्रीभ्यो दद्यान्महेश्वरि ।

वन्ध्यां पुत्रप्रदं देवि नात्र कार्या विचारणा ॥ २६ ॥

Pronunciation

navanītaṃ cābhimantrya strībhyo dadyān maheśvari ।

vandhyāṃ putrapradaṃ devi nātra kāryā vicāraṇā ॥ 26 ॥

Meaning

Oh great Goddess, if freshly churned butter is consecrated with this hymn and given to women, it bestows children upon the barren, without any doubt.

कण्ठे वा वामबाहौ वा योनौ वा धारणाच्छिवे ।

बहुपुत्रवती नारी सुभगा जायते ध्रुवम् ॥ २७ ॥

Pronunciation

kaṇṭhe vā vāmabāhau vā yonau vā dhāraṇāc chive ।

bahuputravatī nārī subhagā jāyate dhruvam ॥ 27 ॥

Meaning

Oh Shiva, if it is worn upon the neck, the left arm, or at the yoni, a woman surely becomes fortunate and blessed with many children.

उग्र उग्रं महदुग्रं स्तवमिदं ललितायाः ।

सुविनीताय शान्ताय दान्तायातिगुणाय च ॥ २८ ॥

Pronunciation

ugra ugraṃ mahadugraṃ stavam idaṃ Lalitayāḥ ।

suvinītāya śāntāya dāntāyātiguṇāya ca ॥ 28 ॥

Meaning

This hymn of Lalita is fierce, extremely ferocious, and supremely powerful. Therefore it should be given only to one who is well disciplined, peaceful, self-controlled and possesses excellent qualities.

भक्ताय ज्येष्ठपुत्राय गुरुभक्तिपराय च ।
भक्तभक्ताय योग्याय भक्तिशक्तिपराय च ॥ २९ ॥

Pronunciation

bhaktāya jyeṣṭhaputrāya
gurubhaktiparāya ca ।

bhaktabhaktāya yogyāya
bhaktiśaktiparāya ca ॥ 29 ॥

Meaning

It should be given to a devotee, to the worthy eldest son, to one devoted to the Guru, to a devotee of devotees, to a qualified recipient, and to one dedicated to both devotion and Shakti.

वेश्यापूजनयुक्ताय कुमारीपूजकाय च ।
दुर्गाभक्ताय शैवाय कामेश्वरप्रजापिने ॥ ३० ॥

Pronunciation

veśyāpūjanayuktāya
kumārīpūjakāya ca ।

durgābhaktāya śaivāya
kāmeśvaraprajāpine ॥ 30 ॥

Meaning

It should be given to one who participates in the prescribed worship of courtesans, to a worshipper of maidens, to a devotee of Durga, to a follower of Shiva and to one who recites the mantra of Kameshvara.

अद्वैतभावयुक्ताय शक्तिभक्तिपराय च ।

प्रदेयं शतनामाख्यं स्वयं ललिताज्ञया ॥ ३१ ॥

Pronunciation

advaitabhāvayuktāya
śaktibhaktiparāya ca ।

pradeyaṃ śatanāmākhyaṃ svayaṃ
Lalitajñayā ॥ 31 ॥

Meaning

By the command of Lalita herself, this hymn of one hundred names is to be given to one established in the non dual view and devoted to the worship of Shakti.

खलाय परतन्त्राय परनिन्दापराय च ।

भ्रष्टाय दुष्टतत्त्वाय परीवादपराय च ॥ ३२ ॥

Pronunciation

khalāya paratantrāya
paranindāparāya ca ।

bhraṣṭāya duṣṭatattvāya
parīvādaparāya ca ॥ 32 ॥

Meaning

It should not be given to a wicked person, one dependent upon others, one devoted to slandering others, one who has fallen from the path, one of corrupt understanding, or one given to malicious criticism.

शिवाभक्ताय दुष्टाय परदाररताय च ।

वेश्यास्त्रीनिन्दकाय च पञ्चमकारनिन्दके ॥ ३३ ॥

Pronunciation

śivābhaktāya duṣṭāya
paradāraratāya ca ।

veśyāstrīnindakāya ca
pañcamakāranindake ॥ 33 ॥

Meaning

It should not be given to one who lacks devotion to Shiva, to the wicked, to one attached to another's wife, to one who reviles women employed in the sacred rites, or to one who condemns the pancamakaras (the 5 Ms - wine, meat, fish, mudra and union) .

न स्तोत्रं दर्शयेद्देवी मम हत्याकरो भवेत् ।

तस्मान्न दापयेद्देवी मनसा कर्मणा गिरा ॥ ३४ ॥

Pronunciation

na stotraṃ darśayed devi mama hatyākaro bhavet ।

tasmān na dāpayed devi manasā karmaṇā girā ॥ 34 ॥

Meaning

O Goddess, one who reveals this hymn improperly becomes as though guilty of slaying me. Therefore it should not be imparted carelessly, whether by thought, deed or speech.

अन्यथा कुरुते यस्तु स क्षीणायुर्भवेद्ध्रुवम् ।

पुत्रहारी च स्त्रीहारी राज्यहारी भवेद्ध्रुवम् ॥ ३५ ॥

Pronunciation

anyathā kurute yastu sa kṣīṇāyur bhaved dhruvam ।

putrahārī ca strīhārī rājyahārī bhaved dhruvam ॥ 35 ॥

Meaning

One who acts otherwise surely suffers a shortened lifespan. He becomes deprived of sons, deprived of his wife and deprived of his position or kingdom.

मन्त्रक्षोभश्च जायते तस्य मृत्युर्भविष्यति ।

क्रमदीक्षायुतानां च सिद्धिर्भवति नान्यथा ॥ ३६ ॥

Pronunciation

mantrakṣobhaś ca jāyate tasya mṛtyur bhaviṣyati ।

kramadīkṣāyutānāṃ ca siddhir bhavati nānyathā ॥ 36 ॥

Meaning

His mantra becomes disturbed and ineffective and death eventually befalls him. Accomplishment arises only for those who possess the proper Krama initiation, and not otherwise.

क्रमदीक्षायुतो देवी क्रमाद्राज्यमवाप्नुयात् ।

क्रमदीक्षासमायुक्तः कल्पोक्तसिद्धिभाग्भवेत् ॥ ३७ ॥

Pronunciation

kramadīkṣāyuto devi kramād
rājyam avāpnuyāt ।

kramadīkṣāsamāyuktaḥ
kalpoktasiddhibhāg bhavet ॥ 37 ॥

Meaning

Oh Goddess, one endowed with Krama initiation gradually attains sovereignty. By possession of such initiation, he becomes a recipient of all the accomplishments described in the scriptures.

विधेर्लिपिं तु सम्मार्ज्य किङ्करत्वं विसृज्य च ।

सर्वसिद्धिमवाप्नोति नात्र कार्या विचारणा ॥ ३८ ॥

Pronunciation

vidher lipiṃ tu sammārjya
kiṅkaratvaṃ visṛjya ca ।

sarvasiddhim avāpnoti nātra kāryā
vicāraṇā ॥ 38 ॥

Meaning

Having wiped away the script of fate and cast off the condition of servitude, one attains every accomplishment, without doubt.

क्रमदीक्षायुतो देवी मम समो न संशयः ।

गोपनीयं गोपनीयं गोपनीयं सदाऽनघे ॥ ३९ ॥

Pronunciation

kramadīkṣāyuto devi mama samo na saṃśayaḥ ।

gopanīyaṃ gopanīyaṃ gopanīyaṃ sadānaghe ॥ 39 ॥

Meaning

The practitioner endowed with Krama initiation becomes equal to me, without any doubt. Therefore this teaching must be kept forever a secret, always a secret like the secret of secrets.

स दीक्षितः सुखी साधुः सत्यवादी जितेन्द्रियः ।

स वेदवक्ता स्वाध्यायी सर्वानन्दपरायणः ॥ ४० ॥

Pronunciation

sa dīkṣitaḥ sukhī sādhuḥ satyavādī jitendriyaḥ ।

sa vedavaktā svādhyāyī sarvānandaparāyaṇaḥ ॥ 40 ॥

Meaning

The initiated practitioner becomes happy, virtuous, truthful and master of his senses. He becomes a knower and expounder of sacred wisdom, devoted to study, and established in bliss.

स्वस्मिन् ललितां सम्भाव्य पूजयेज्जगदम्बिकाम् ।

त्रैलोक्यविजयी भूयान्नात्र कार्या विचारणा ॥ ४१ ॥

Pronunciation

svasmin Lalitaṃ sambhāvya pūjayej jagadambikām ।

trailokyavijayī bhūyān nātra kāryā vicāraṇā ॥ 41 ॥

Meaning

Recognising Lalita within oneself, one should worship the mother of the Universe. Such a practitioner becomes victorious throughout the three worlds, without doubt.

गुरुरूपं शिवं ध्यात्वा शिवरूपं गुरुं स्मरेत् ।

सदाशिवः स एव स्यान्नात्र कार्या विचारणा ॥ ४२ ॥

Pronunciation

gururūpaṃ śivaṃ dhyātvā
śivarūpaṃ guruṃ smaret ।

sadāśivaḥ sa eva syān nātra kāryā
vicāraṇā ॥ 42 ॥

Meaning

Having meditated upon Shiva in the form of the Guru, and remembering the Guru as the very form of Shiva, the practitioner himself becomes Sadashiva, without any doubt.

इति चतुर्थः पटलः ॥

iti caturthaḥ paṭalaḥ ॥

This ends the Fourth Chapter, the Phala Patala or Chapter of Benefits, in the Lalita Tripura Sundari Shodashi Tantra.

Chapter Five

Srividya Patala

The Chapter of Revelation

ॐ तिस्त्रः पुरास्त्रिपथा विश्वचर्षणा अत्राकथा
अक्षराः सन्निविष्टाः ।
अधिष्ठायैना अजरा पुराणी महत्तरा महिमा देवतानाम्
॥ १॥

Pronunciation

oṃ tisraḥ purās tripathā viśvacarṣaṇā atrākathā akṣarāḥ sanniviṣṭāḥ ।

adhiṣṭhāyainā ajarā purāṇī mahattarā mahimā devatānām ॥ 1 ॥

Meaning

The three cities and the three paths, revered by all beings are established here together with their imperishable principles. Presiding over them is the ancient, undecaying one, whose greatness surpasses that of all the gods.

नवयोनिर्नवचक्राणि दधिरे नवैव योगा नव योगिन्यश्च
।
नवानां चक्रा अधिनाथाः स्योना नव मुद्रा नव भद्रा
महीनाम् ॥ २॥

Pronunciation

navayonir navacakrāṇi dadhire
navaiva yogā nava yoginyaś ca ।

navānāṃ cakrā adhināthāḥ syonā
nava mudrā nava bhadrā mahīnām
॥ 2 ॥

Meaning

The nine yonis, the nine chakras, the nine yogas, and the nine Yoginis are established therein along with the nine rulers of the chakras, the nine mudras, and the nine auspicious powers of the Earth.

एका सा आसीत् प्रथमा सा
नवासीदासोनविंशादासोनत्रिंशत् ।
चत्वारिंशादथ तिस्त्रः समिधा उशतीरिव मातरो मा
विशन्तु ॥ ३॥

Pronunciation

ekā sā āsīt prathamā sā navāsīd
āsonaviṃśād āsonatriṃśat ।

catvāriṃśād atha tisraḥ samidhā
uśatīr iva mātaro mā viśantu ॥ 3 ॥

Meaning

She was the one in the beginning, and then she became Nine, then nineteen, then twenty nine, and then forty. May those radiant powers, like nurturing mothers and sacred offerings enter into me.

ऊर्ध्वज्वलज्ज्वलनं ज्योतिरग्रे तमो वै तिरश्चीनमजरं
तद्रजोऽभूत् ।
आनन्दनं मोदनं ज्योतिरिन्दो रेता उ वै मण्डला
मण्डयन्ति ॥ ४॥

Pronunciation

ūrdhvajvalajvalanaṃ jyotir agre tamo vai tiraścīnam ajaraṃ tad rajo'bhūt ।

ānandanaṃ modanaṃ jyotir indo retā u vai maṇḍalā maṇḍayanti ॥ 4 ॥

Meaning

In the beginning there was the upward blazing light, and then arose darkness extending across, and from it emerged the subtle creative principle. Bliss, delight and the lunar radiance adorn the circles of manifestation with their generative power.

तिस्रश्च रेखाः सदनानि
भूमेस्त्रिविष्टपास्त्रिगुणास्त्रिप्रकाराः ।
एतत्पुरं पूरकं पूरकाणामत्र प्रथते मदनो मदन्या ॥
५॥

Pronunciation

tisraś ca rekhāḥ sadanāni bhūmes
triviṣṭapās triguṇās triprakārāḥ ।

etat puraṃ pūrakaṃ pūrakāṇām
atra prathate madano madanyā ॥ 5
॥

Meaning

The three lines, the abodes of the earth, the three heavens, the three gunas and the threefold divisions are all contained herein. This sacred city fulfils all fulfillments, and here the Lord of Desire shines forth together with his beloved.

मदन्तिका मानिनी मंगला च सुभगा च सा सुन्दरी
सिद्धिमत्ता ।
लज्जा मतिस्तुष्टिरिष्टा च पुष्टा लक्ष्मीरुमा ललिता
लालपन्ती ॥ ६॥

Pronunciation

madantikā māninī maṅgalā ca
subhagā ca sā sundarī siddhimattā ।

lajjā matis tuṣṭir iṣṭā ca puṣṭā
lakṣmīr umā Lalita lālapantī ॥ 6 ॥

Meaning

She is Madantika, Manini, Mangala, Subhaga, Sundari, and the bestower of Siddhi. She is Modesty, Wisdom, Contentment, Fulfillment, Prosperity, Lakshmi, Uma, and Lalita herself.

इमां विज्ञाय सुधया मदन्ती परिसृता तर्पयन्तः स्वपीठम् ।
नाकस्य पृष्ठे वसन्ति परं धाम त्रैपुरं चाविशन्ति ॥ ७॥

Pronunciation

imāṃ vijñāya sudhayā madantī parisṛtā tarpayantaḥ svapīṭham ।

nākasya pṛṣṭhe vasanti paraṃ dhāma traipuraṃ cāviśanti ॥ 7 ॥

Meaning

Knowing this Goddess and delighting in her nectar while satisfying her at their own sacred seat, practitioners dwell upon the summit of heaven and enter the supreme abode of Tripura.

कामो योनिः कामकला व्रजपाणिर्गुहा हसा
मातरिश्वाभ्रमिन्द्रः ।
पुनर्गुहा सकला मायया च पूरूच्येषा
विश्वमातादिविद्या ॥ ८॥

Pronunciation

kāmo yoniḥ kāmakalā vrajapāṇir
guhā hasā mātariśvābhram indraḥ ।

punar guhā sakalā māyayā ca
pūrūcyeṣā viśvamātādividyā ॥ 8 ॥

Meaning

Kama is her source, Kamakala her essence. Hidden and mysterious, she appears through the powers of creation and illusion. She is the Mother of the Universe and the Primordial Knowledge.

षष्ठं सप्तममथ वह्निसारथिमस्या मूलत्रिक्रमा देशयन्तः ।
कथ्यं कविं कल्पकं काममीशं तुष्टुवांसो अमृतत्वं भजन्ते ॥ ९॥

Pronunciation

ṣaṣṭhaṃ saptamam atha vahnisārathim asyā mūlatrikramā deśayantaḥ ।

kathyaṃ kaviṃ kalpakaṃ kāmam īśaṃ tuṣṭuvāṃso amṛtatvaṃ bhajante ॥ 9 ॥

Meaning

Those who understand and teach the hidden stages of her essential progression, praising the Seer, the Creator, Kama and the Lord, attain immortality.

त्रिविष्टपं त्रिमुखं विश्वमातुर्नवरेखाः स्वरमध्यं तदीले
।
बृहत्तिथिर्दशा पञ्चादि नित्या सा षोडशी पुरमध्यं
बिभर्ति ॥ १०॥

Pronunciation

triviṣṭapaṃ trimukhaṃ viśvamātur
navarekhāḥ svaramadhyaṃ tad īle ।

bṛhattithir daśā pañcādi nityā sā
ṣoḍaśī puramadhyaṃ bibharti ॥ 10
॥

Meaning

I praise that central mystery of the Universal Mother, marked by nine lines and established in the midst of sacred sound. The fifteen Nitya goddesses culminate in the Sixteenth, Shodashi, who abides at the centre of the City.

यद्वा मण्डलाद्वा स्तनबिंबमेकं मुखं चाधस्त्रीणि गुहा सदनानि ।
कामी कलां काम्यरूपां विदित्वा नरो जायते कामरूपश्च काम्यः ॥ ११॥

Pronunciation

yadvā maṇḍalād vā stanabiṃbam ekaṃ mukhaṃ cādhas trīṇi guhā sadanāni ।

kāmī kalāṃ kāmyarūpāṃ viditvā naro jāyate kāmarūpaś ca kāmyaḥ ॥ 11 ॥

Meaning

Whether contemplated as a mandala or as the sacred form of the Goddess, with its hidden centres below, the practitioner who realises the Kamakala and her desirable form becomes himself the embodiment of divine desire and attraction.

परिसृतम् झषमाद्यं फलं च भक्तानि योनीः
सुपरिष्कृताश्च ।
निवेदयन्देवतायै महत्यै स्वात्मीकृते सुकृते सिद्धिमेति
॥ १२॥

Pronunciation

parisṛtam jhaṣamādyaṃ phalaṃ ca bhaktāni yonīḥ supariṣkṛtāś ca ।

nivedayan devatāyai mahatyai svātmīkṛte sukṛte siddhim eti ॥ 12 ॥

Meaning

Offering fish, fruits and other consecrated substances, together with the purified yonis, to the Great Goddess, and realising her as one's own Self, the practitioner attains accomplishment.

सृण्येव सितया विश्वचर्षणिः पाशेनैव
प्रतिबध्नात्यभीकाम् ।
इषुभिः पञ्चभिर्धनुषा च विध्यत्यादिशक्तिररुणा
विश्वजन्या ॥ १३॥

Pronunciation

sṛṇyeva sitayā viśvacarṣaṇiḥ
pāśenaiva pratibadhnāty abhīkām ।

iṣubhiḥ pañcabhir dhanuṣā ca
vidhyaty ādiśaktir aruṇā viśvajanyā
॥ 13 ॥

Meaning

Like a shining hook she draws all beings toward herself, with her noose she binds those whom she desires. With her bow and five arrows, the primordial crimson Shakti, Mother of the Universe, pierces and governs all creation.

भगः शक्तिर्भगवान्काम ईश उभा दाताराविह
सौभगानाम् ।
समप्रधानौ समसत्वौ समोजौ तयोः शक्तिरजरा
विश्वयोनिः ॥ १४॥

Pronunciation

bhagaḥ śaktir bhagavān kāma īśa
ubhau dātārāv iha saubhagānām ।

samapradhānau samasattvau
samojau tayoḥ śaktir ajarā
viśvayoniḥ ॥ 14 ॥

Meaning

Shakti is the Divine Womb (bhaga), and Kama is the Divine Lord. Together they are the bestowers of all auspiciousness. Equal in status, equal in essence, and equal in power, their eternal union is the imperishable Source of the Universe.

परिस्रुता हविषा भावितेन प्रसङ्कोचे गलिते वैमनस्कः
।
शर्वः सर्वस्य जगतो विधाता धर्ता हर्ता
विश्वरूपत्वमेति ॥ १५॥

Pronunciation

parisrutā haviṣā bhāvitena
prasaṅkoce galite vaimanaskaḥ ।

śarvaḥ sarvasya jagato vidhātā
dhartā hartā viśvarūpatvam eti ॥
15 ॥

Meaning

When the offering has been properly consecrated and the contracted state of mind dissolves away, the practitioner realises Sarva (Shiva) as the Creator, Sustainer, and Dissolver of the entire universe, and attains identity with the Cosmic Form.

इयं महोपनिषत्त्रैपुर्या यामक्षरं परमो गीर्भिरीट्टे ।
एषर्ग्यजुः परमेतच्च सामायमथर्वेयमन्या च विद्या ॥
१६॥

Pronunciation

iyaṃ mahopaniṣat traipuryā yām akṣaraṃ paramo gīrbhir īṭṭe ।

eṣar gyajuḥ param etac ca sāmāyam atharveyam anyā ca vidyā ॥ 16 ॥

Meaning

This is the Great Upanishad of Tripura. The Supreme Imperishable Reality praised by the sacred hymns is revealed herein. It is the essence of the Rig, Yajur, Sama, and Atharva Vedas, and of every other sacred knowledge.

इति पञ्चमः पटलः ॥

iti pañcamaḥ paṭalaḥ ॥

This ends the Fifth Chapter, the Srividya Patala or Chapter of Revelation, in the Lalita Tripura Sundari Shodashi Tantra.

Chapter Six

Stotram Patala

The Chapter of Litany

ॐ श्रीमाता श्रीमहाराज्ञी श्रीमत्-सिंहासनेश्वरी ।

चिदग्नि-कुण्ड-सम्भूता देवकार्य-समुद्यता ॥ १॥

Pronunciation

oṃ śrīmātā śrīmahārājñī
śrīmatsiṃhāsaneśvarī ।

cidagnikuṇḍasambhūtā
devakāryasamudyatā ॥ 1 ॥

Meaning

She is the Holy Mother, the Great Empress, enthroned upon the glorious lion-seat and arising from the sacred fire of consciousness, She manifests for the accomplishment of the divine purpose.

उद्यद्भानु-सहस्राभा चतुर्बाहु-समन्विता ।

रागस्वरूप-पाशाढ्या क्रोधाकाराङ्कुशोज्ज्वला ॥ २॥

Pronunciation

udyadbhānu-sahasrābhā caturbāhu-samanvitā ।

rāgasvarūpa-pāśāḍhyā krodhākārāṅkuśojjvalā ॥ 2 ॥

Meaning

She shines like a thousand rising suns and is endowed with four arms while holding the noose of loving attraction and the goad of divine power, She governs all beings.

मनोरूपेक्षु-कोदण्डा पञ्चतन्मात्र-सायका ।

निजारुण-प्रभापूर-मज्जद्ब्रह्माण्ड-मण्डला ॥ ३॥

Pronunciation

manorūpekṣu-kodaṇḍā
pañcatanmātra-sāyakā ।

nijāruṇa-prabhāpūra-
majjadbrahmāṇḍamaṇḍalā ॥ 3 ॥

Meaning

Her sugarcane bow is the mind itself, and Her arrows are the five subtle elements. The universe is immersed in the flood of Her crimson radiance.

चम्पकाशोक-पुन्नाग-सौगन्धिक-लसत्कचा ।
कुरुविन्दमणि-श्रेणी-कनत्कोटीर-मण्डिता ॥ ४॥

Pronunciation

campakāśoka-punnāga-
saugandhika-lasatkacā ।

kuruvindamaṇiśreṇī-kanatkoṭīra-
maṇḍitā ॥ 4 ॥

Meaning

Her hair is adorned with fragrant campaka, ashoka, and punnaga blossoms while Her crown shines with rows of brilliant rubies.

अष्टमीचन्द्र-विभ्राज-दलिकस्थल-शोभिता ।

मुखचन्द्र-कलङ्काभ-मृगनाभि-विशेषका ॥ ५॥

Pronunciation

aṣṭamīcandra-vibhrāja-dalikasthala-śobhitā ।

mukhacandra-kalaṅkābha-mṛganābhi-viśeṣakā ॥ 5 ॥

Meaning

Her forehead shines like the crescent moon of the eighth lunar day and a musk-mark beautifies Her face like the dark spot upon the moon.

वदनस्मर-माङ्गल्य-गृहतोरण-चिल्लिका ।

वक्त्रलक्ष्मी-परीवाह-चलन्मीनाभ-लोचना ॥ ६॥

Pronunciation

vadanasmara-māṅgalya-gṛhatoraṇa-cillikā ।

vaktralakṣmī-parīvāha-calanmīnābha-locanā ॥ 6 ॥

Meaning

Her eyebrows resemble auspicious archways to the mansion of Love. Her eyes move gracefully like fish swimming in the stream of beauty flowing from Her face.

नवचम्पक-पुष्पाभ-नासादण्ड-विराजिता ।

ताराकान्ति-तिरस्कारि-नासाभरण-भासुरा ॥ ७॥

Pronunciation

navacampaka-puṣpābha-nāsādaṇḍa-virājitā ।

tārākānti-tiraskāri-nāsābharaṇa-bhāsurā ॥ 7 ॥

Meaning

Her nose is as delicate and radiant as a fresh campaka blossom and the brilliance of Her nose ornament surpasses the splendor of the stars.

kadambamañjarī-kḷpta-
karṇapūra-manoharā ।

tāṭaṅka-yugalī-bhūta-tapanoḍupa-
maṇḍalā ॥ 8 ॥

Pronunciation

kadambamañjarī-kḷpta-karṇapūra-
manoharā ।

tāṭaṅka-yugalī-bhūta-tapanoḍupa-
maṇḍalā ॥ 8 ॥

Meaning

She enchants with earrings fashioned like clusters of kadamba flowers and Her great ear ornaments symbolise the sun and moon.

पद्मराग-शिलादर्श-परिभावि-कपोलभूः ।

नवविद्रुम-बिम्बश्री-न्यक्कारि-रदनच्छदा ॥ ९॥

Pronunciation

padmarāga-śilādarśa-paribhāvi-kapolabhūḥ ।

navavidruma-bimbaśrī-nyakkāri-radanacchadā ॥ 9 ॥

Meaning

Her cheeks outshine polished ruby mirrors and Her lips surpass the beauty of fresh coral and ripe bimba fruit.

शुद्ध-विद्याङ्कुराकार-द्विजपङ्क्ति-द्वयोज्ज्वला ।

कर्पूर-वीटिकामोद-समाकर्षि-दिगन्तरा ॥ १०॥

Pronunciation

śuddhavidyāṅkurākāra-dvijapaṅkti-dvayojjvalā ।

karpūra-vīṭikāmoda-samākarṣi-digantarā ॥ 10 ॥

Meaning

Her rows of teeth shine like sprouts of pure knowledge and the fragrances of camphor and betel from Her mouth attracts from all directions.

निज-सल्लाप-माधुर्य-विनिर्भर्त्सित-कच्छपी ।

मन्दस्मित-प्रभापूर-मज्जत्कामेश-मानसा ॥ ११॥

Pronunciation

nijasallāpa-mādhurya-
vinirbhartsita-kacchapī ।

mandasmita-prabhāpūra-
majjatkāmeśa-mānasā ॥ 11 ॥

Meaning

The sweetness of Her speech surpasses the music of the vina and The mind of Kameshvara is immersed in the radiance of Her gentle smile.

अनाकलित-सादृश्य-चिबुकश्री-विराजिता ।

कामेश-बद्ध-माङ्गल्य-सूत्र-शोभित-कन्धरा ॥ १२॥

Pronunciation

anākalita-sādṛśya-cibukaśrī-virājitā
।

kāmeśa-baddha-māṅgalya-sūtra-
śobhita-kandharā ॥ 12 ॥

Meaning

Her chin possesses incomparable beauty and Her neck is adorned with the auspicious marriage necklace tied by Kamesha.

कनकाङ्गद-केयूर-कमनीय-भुजान्विता ।

रत्नग्रैवेय-चिन्ताक-लोल-मुक्ता-फलान्विता ॥ १३॥

Pronunciation

kanakāṅgada-keyūra-kamanīya-bhujānvitā ।

ratnagraiveya-cintāka-lola-muktā-phalānvitā ॥ 13 ॥

Meaning

Her graceful arms are adorned with golden armlets and bracelets as jewel necklaces and swinging pearls enhance Her splendour.

कामेश्वर-प्रेमरत्न-मणि-प्रतिपण-स्तनी ।

नाभ्यालवाल-रोमालि-लता-फल-कुचद्वयी ॥ १४॥

Pronunciation

kāmeśvara-premaratna-maṇi-
pratipaṇa-stanī ।

nābhyālavāla-romāli-Lata-phala-
kucadvayī ॥ 14 ॥

Meaning

Her breasts are the priceless exchange for Kameshvara's jewel of love as they are like twin fruits growing upon the vine of fine hair rising from Her navel.

लक्ष्यरोम-लताधारता-समुन्नेय-मध्यमा ।

स्तनभार-दलन्मध्य-पट्टबन्ध-वलित्रया ॥ १५॥

Pronunciation

lakṣyaroma-Latadhāratā-samunneya-madhyamā ।

stanabhāra-dalanmadhya-paṭṭabandha-valitrayā ॥ 15 ॥

Meaning

Her slender waist seems sustained only by the delicate line of hair above it as three folds adorn Her middle, formed by the weight of Her breasts.

अरुणारुण-कौसुम्भ-वस्त्र-भास्वत्-कटीतटी ।

रत्न-किङ्किणिका-रम्य-रशना-दाम-भूषिता ॥ १६॥

Pronunciation

aruṇāruṇa-kausumbha-vastra-bhāsvat-kaṭītaṭī ।

ratna-kiṅkiṇikā-ramya-raśanā-dāma-bhūṣitā ॥ 16 ॥

Meaning

Her hips are wrapped in garments glowing with a crimson hue and a jewelled girdle adorned with tinkling bells beautifies Her waist.

कामेश-ज्ञात-सौभाग्य-मार्दवोरु-द्वयान्विता ।

माणिक्य-मुकुटाकार-जानुद्वय-विराजिता ॥ १७॥

Pronunciation

kāmeśa-jñāta-saubhāgya-
mārdavoru-dvayānvitā ।

māṇikya-mukuṭākāra-jānudvaya-
virājitā ॥ 17 ॥

Meaning

The softness and beauty of Her thighs are known only to Kamesha and Her knees shine like crowns fashioned from rubies.

इन्द्रगोप-परिक्षिप्त-स्मरतूणाभ-जङ्घिका ।

गूढगुल्फा कूर्मपृष्ठ-जयिष्णु-प्रपदान्विता ॥ १८॥

Pronunciation

indragopa-parikṣipta-
smaratūṇābha-jaṅghikā ।

gūḍhagulphā kūrmapṛṣṭha-jayiṣṇu-
prapadānvitā ॥ 18 ॥

Meaning

Her calves resemble Love's quiver adorned with red indragopa insects as Her ankles are concealed, and Her feet are beautifully arched like a tortoise's back.

नख-दीधिति-संछन्न-नमज्जन-तमोगुणा ।

पदद्वय-प्रभाजाल-पराकृत-सरोरुहा ॥ १९॥

Pronunciation

nakhadīdhiti-saṃchanna-
namajjana-tamoguṇā ।

padadvaya-prabhājāla-parākṛta-
saroruhā ॥ 19 ॥

Meaning

The radiance of Her toenails dispels the darkness of those who bow before Her and The brilliance of Her feet surpasses the beauty of lotuses.

सिञ्जान-मणिमञ्जीर-मण्डित-श्री-पदाम्बुजा ।

मराली-मन्दगमना महालावण्य-शेवधिः ॥ २०॥

Pronunciation

siñjāna-maṇimañjīra-maṇḍita-śrī-padāmbujā ।

marālī-mandagamanā mahālāvaṇya-śevadhiḥ ॥ 20 ॥

Meaning

Her lotus feet are adorned with tinkling jewelled anklets as She walks gracefully like a swan and is the very treasure house of beauty.

सर्वारुणाऽनवद्याङ्गी सर्वाभरण-भूषिता ।

शिव-कामेश्वराङ्कस्था शिवा स्वाधीन-वल्लभा ॥

२१॥

Pronunciation

sarvāruṇānavadyāṅgī
sarvābharaṇa-bhūṣitā ।

śiva-kāmeśvarāṅkasthā śivā
svādhīna-vallabhā ॥ 21 ॥

Meaning

Entirely rosy in complexion and flawless in every limb, She is adorned with all ornaments and Seated upon the lap of Shiva-Kameshvara, She holds Her beloved completely under Her influence.

सुमेरु-मध्य-शृङ्गस्था श्रीमन्नगर-नायिका ।

चिन्तामणि-गृहान्तस्था पञ्च-ब्रह्मासन-स्थिता ॥

२२॥

Pronunciation

sumeru-madhya-śṛṅgasthā
śrīmannagara-nāyikā ।

cintāmaṇi-gṛhāntasthā
pañcabrahmāsana-sthitā ॥ 22 ॥

Meaning

She resides upon the central peak of Mount Meru as the Queen of the sacred city and Dwelling in the Chintamaṇi palace, She is seated upon the throne formed by the five Brahmas.

महापद्माटवी-संस्था कदम्बवन-वासिनी ।

सुधासागर-मध्यस्था कामाक्षी कामदायिनी ॥ २३॥

Pronunciation

mahāpadmāṭavī-saṃsthā
kadambavana-vāsinī ।

sudhāsāgara-madhyasthā kāmākṣī
kāmadāyinī ॥ 23 ॥

Meaning

She dwells within the great lotus forest and in the kadamba grove and Residing amidst the ocean of nectar, Kamakshi grants all worthy desires.

देवर्षि-गण-संघात-स्तूयमानात्म-वैभवा ।

भण्डासुर-वधोद्युक्त-शक्तिसेना-समन्विता ॥ २४॥

Pronunciation

devarṣi-gaṇa-saṃghāta-
stūyamānātma-vaibhavā ।

bhaṇḍāsura-vadhodyukta-śaktisenā-
samanvitā ॥ 24 ॥

Meaning

Her glory is praised by hosts of divine sages and She is attended by an army of Shaktis prepared for the destruction of Bhandasura.

सम्पत्करी-समारूढ-सिन्धुर-व्रज-सेविता ।

अश्वारूढाधिष्ठिताश्व-कोटि-कोटिभिरावृता ॥ २५॥

Pronunciation

sampatkarī-samārūḍha-sindhura-vraja-sevitā ।

aśvārūḍhādhiṣṭhitāśva-koṭi-koṭibhirāvṛtā ॥ 25 ॥

Meaning

She is served by regiments of elephants commanded by Sampatkari and She is surrounded by countless cavalry forces led by Ashvarudha.

चक्रराज-रथारूढ-सर्वायुध-परिष्कृता ।

गेयचक्र-रथारूढ-मन्त्रिणी-परिसेविता ॥ २६॥

Pronunciation

cakrarāja-rathārūḍha-sarvāyudha-pariṣkṛtā ।

geyacakra-rathārūḍha-mantriṇī-parisevitā ॥ 26 ॥

Meaning

Mounted upon the royal chariot of the Sricakra and equipped with every divine weapon, She is attended by Mantrini, who rides the Geya-cakra chariot.

किरिचक्र-रथारूढ-दण्डनाथा-पुरस्कृता ।

ज्वाला-मालिनिकाक्षिप्त-वह्निप्राकार-मध्यगा ॥ २७॥

Pronunciation

kiricakra-rathārūḍha-daṇḍanāthā-puraskṛtā ।

jvālā-mālinikākṣipta-vahniprākāra-madhyagā ॥ 27 ॥

Meaning

Preceded by Dandanatha riding the Kiri-cakra chariot, She abides within a fortress of fire created by Jvalamalini.

भण्डसैन्य-वधोद्युक्त-शक्ति-विक्रम-हर्षिता ।

नित्या-पराक्रमाटोप-निरीक्षण-समुत्सुका ॥ २८॥

Pronunciation

bhaṇḍasainya-vadhodyukta-śakti-vikrama-harṣitā ।

nityā-parākramāṭopa-nirīkṣaṇa-samutsukā ॥ 28 ॥

Meaning

She rejoices in the valour of Her Shakti forces engaged in destroying Bhanda's army and eagerly watches the heroic exploits of the Nitya Deities.

भण्डपुत्र-वधोद्युक्त-बाला-विक्रम-नन्दिता ।

मन्त्रिण्यम्बा-विरचित-विषङ्ग-वध-तोषिता ॥ २९॥

Pronunciation

bhaṇḍaputra-vadhodyukta-bālā-vikrama-nanditā ।

mantriṇyambā-viracita-viṣaṅga-vadha-toṣitā ॥ 29 ॥

Meaning

She delights in the heroism of Bala, who destroys Bhanda's sons, and is pleased by Mantrini's slaying of Visanga.

विशुक्र-प्राणहरण-वाराही-वीर्य-नन्दिता ।

कामेश्वर-मुखालोक-कल्पित-श्रीगणेश्वरा ॥ ३०॥

Pronunciation

viśukra-prāṇaharaṇa-vārāhī-vīrya-nanditā ।

kāmeśvara-mukhāloka-kalpita-śrīgaṇeśvarā ॥ 30 ॥

Meaning

She rejoices in Varahi's destruction of Visukra and manifests Ganesha through a glance exchanged with Kameshvara.

महागणेश-निर्भिन्न-विघ्नयन्त्र-प्रहर्षिता ।
भण्डासुरेन्द्र-निर्मुक्त-शस्त्र-प्रत्यस्त्र-वर्षिणी ॥ ३१॥

Pronunciation

mahāgaṇeśa-nirbhinna-
vighnayantra-praharṣitā ।

bhaṇḍāsurendra-nirmukta-śastra-
pratyastra-varṣiṇī ॥ 31 ॥

Meaning

She rejoices when Mahaganesha shatters the enemy's obstacle machines and counters Bhandasura's weapons with divine missiles.

करांगुलि-नखोत्पन्न-नारायण-दशाकृतिः ।

महा-पाशुपतास्त्राग्नि-निर्दग्धासुर-सैनिका ॥ ३२॥

Pronunciation

karāṅguli-nakhotpanna-nārāyaṇa-daśākṛtiḥ ।

mahāpāśupatāstrāgni-nirdagdhāsura-sainikā ॥ 32 ॥

Meaning

From the nails of Her fingers arise the ten forms of Narayana and By the fire of the Mahapasupata weapon, She burns the armies of the demons.

कामेश्वरास्त्र-निर्दग्ध-सभण्डासुर-शून्यका ।

ब्रह्मोपेन्द्र-महेन्द्रादि-देव-संस्तुत-वैभवा ॥ ३३॥

Pronunciation

kāmeśvarāstra-nirdagdha-
sabhaṇḍāsura-śūnyakā ।

brahmopendra-mahendrādi-deva-
saṃstuta-vaibhavā ॥ 33 ॥

Meaning

By the Kamesvara missile, She annihilates Bhandasura and his hosts. Her glory is praised by Brahma, Vishu, Indra and the gods.

हर-नेत्राग्नि-संदग्ध-काम-सञ्जीवनौषधिः ।

श्रीमद्वाग्भव-कूटैक-स्वरूप-मुख-पङ्कजा ॥ ३४॥

Pronunciation

hara-netrāgni-saṃdagdha-kāma-sañjīvanauṣadhiḥ ।

śrīmadvāgbhava-kūṭaika-svarūpa-mukha-paṅkajā ॥ 34 ॥

Meaning

She is the elixir that restores Kama after he was burned by Shiva's third eye and Her lotus face embodies the Vagbhava-kuta of the Srividya mantra.

कण्ठाधः-कटि-पर्यन्त-मध्यकूट-स्वरूपिणी ।

शक्ति-कूटैकतापन्न-कट्यधोभाग-धारिणी ॥ ३५॥

Pronunciation

kaṇṭhādhaḥ-kaṭi-paryanta-
madhyakūṭa-svarūpiṇī ।

śaktikūṭaikatāpanna-
kaṭyadhobhāga-dhāriṇī ॥ 35 ॥

Meaning

From neck to waist She is the embodiment of the Madhya-kuṭa, below the waist She manifests the Shakti-kūṭa of the Srividya mantra.

मूल-मन्त्रात्मिका मूलकूटत्रय-कलेवरा ।

कुलामृतैक-रसिका कुलसंकेत-पालिनी ॥ ३६॥

Pronunciation

mūlamantrātmikā mūlakūṭatraya-kalevarā ।

kulāmṛtaika-rasikā kulasaṃketa-pālinī ॥ 36 ॥

Meaning

She is the essence of the root mantra and whose body is formed by its three kutas as She delights in the nectar of Kula and preserves its sacred mysteries.

कुलाङ्गना कुलान्तस्था कौलिनी कुलयोगिनी ।

अकुला समयान्तस्था समयाचार-तत्परा ॥ ३७॥

Pronunciation

kulāṅganā kulāntasthā kaulinī kulayoginī ।

akulā samayāntasthā samayācāra-tatparā ॥ 37 ॥

Meaning

She is the noble Lady of Kula, dwelling within Kula, the Kaulini, and the Yogini of Kula and yet She transcends Kula and abides in the Samaya tradition.

मूलाधारैक-निलया ब्रह्मग्रन्थि-विभेदिनी ।

मणि-पूरान्तरुदिता विष्णुग्रन्थि-विभेदिनी ॥ ३८॥

Pronunciation

mūlādhāraika-nilayā
brahmagranthi-vibhedinī ।

maṇipūrāntaruditā viṣṇugranthi-
vibhedinī ॥ 38 ॥

Meaning

Residing in the Muladhara, She pierces the Brahma-granthi and Rising through Maṇipura, She breaks the Vishnu-granthi.

आज्ञा-चक्रान्तरालस्था रुद्रग्रन्थि-विभेदिनी ।

सहस्राराम्बुजारूढा सुधा-साराभिवर्षिणी ॥ ३९॥

Pronunciation

ājñācakrāntarālasthā rudragranthi-vibhedinī ।

sahasrārāmbujārūḍhā sudhāsārābhivarṣiṇī ॥ 39 ॥

Meaning

Abiding within the Ajna-cakra, She breaks the Rudra-granthi and ascending to the thousand-petalled lotus, She showers streams of nectar.

तडिल्लता-समरुचिः षट्चक्रोपरि-संस्थिता ।

महासक्तिः कुण्डलिनी बिसतन्तु-तनीयसी ॥ ४०॥

Pronunciation

taḍilLata-samarucih ṣaṭcakropari-saṃsthitā ।

mahāśaktiḥ kuṇḍalinī bisatantu-tanīyasī ॥ 40 ॥

Meaning

Radiant like a streak of lightning and established above the six chakras, She is the great Kundalini Shakti, subtler than the finest lotus fibre.

भवानी भावनागम्या भवारण्य-कुठारिका ।

भद्रप्रिया भद्रमूर्तिर्भक्त-सौभाग्यदायिनी ॥ ४१॥

Pronunciation

bhavānī bhāvanāgamyā
bhavāraṇya-kuṭhārikā ।

bhadrapriyā bhadramūrtirbhakta-
saubhāgyadāyinī ॥ 41 ॥

Meaning

She is Bhavani, attained through contemplation, and the axe that cuts down the forest of worldly existence as She bestows auspiciousness and fortune upon devotees.

भक्तिप्रिया भक्तिगम्या भक्तिवश्या भयापहा ।

शाम्भवी शारदाराध्या शर्वाणी शर्मदायिनी ॥ ४२॥

Pronunciation

bhaktipriyā bhaktigamyā
bhaktivaśyā bhayāpahā ।

śāmbhavī śāradārādhyā śarvāṇī
śarmadāyinī ॥ 42 ॥

Meaning

She loves devotion, is attained through devotion, and is moved by devotion and She removes fear and grants peace and blessedness.

शाङ्करी श्रीकरी साध्वी शरच्चन्द्र-निभानना ।
शातोदरी शान्तिमती निराधारा निरञ्जना ॥ ४३॥

Pronunciation

śāṅkarī śrīkarī sādhvī śaraccandra-nibhānanā ।

śātodarī śāntimatī nirādhārā nirañjanā ॥ 43 ॥

Meaning

She is Shankara's power, the giver of prosperity, virtuous and pure. Her face shines like the autumn moon, She is serene, unsupported and stainless.

निर्लेपा निर्मला नित्या निराकारा निराकुला ।

निर्गुणा निष्कला शान्ता निष्कामा निरुपप्लवा ॥
४४॥

Pronunciation

nirlēpā nirmalā nityā nirākārā nirākulā ।

nirguṇā niṣkalā śāntā niṣkāmā nirupaplavā ॥ 44 ॥

Meaning

Untainted, pure, eternal, formless, and free from disturbance, She transcends all qualities, remains ever peaceful, desire-less, and changeless.

नित्यमुक्ता निर्विकारा निष्प्रपञ्चा निराश्रया ।

नित्यशुद्धा नित्यबुद्धा निरवद्या निरन्तरा ॥ ४५॥

Pronunciation

nityamuktā nirvikārā niṣprapañcā nirāśrayā ।

nityaśuddhā nityabuddhā niravadyā nirantarā ॥ 45 ॥

Meaning

Ever free and unchanging, beyond the manifested universe and dependent on none, She is eternally pure, aware, flawless, and continuous.

निष्कारणा निष्कलङ्का निरुपाधिर्निरीश्वरा ।

नीरागा रागमथनी निर्मदा मदनाशिनी ॥ ४६॥

Pronunciation

niṣkāraṇā niṣkalaṅkā
nirupādhirnirīśvarā ।

nīrāgā rāgamathanī nirmadā
madanāśinī ॥ 46 ॥

Meaning

She exists without cause, free from blemish and limitation, transcending even lordships and free from attachment, She destroys attachment, pride and delusion.

निश्चिन्ता निरहंकारा निर्मोहा मोहनाशिनी ।

निर्ममा ममताहन्त्री निष्पापा पापनाशिनी ॥ ४७॥

Pronunciation

niścintā nirahaṃkārā nirmohā mohanāśinī ।

nirmamā mamatāhantrī niṣpāpā pāpanāśinī ॥ 47 ॥

Meaning

Free from anxiety, ego, and delusion, She destroys ignorance and Possessing no sense of possession, She removes attachment and destroys sin.

निष्क्रोधा क्रोधशमनी निर्लोभा लोभनाशिनी ।

निःसंशया संशयघ्नी निर्भवा भवनाशिनी ॥ ४८॥

Pronunciation

niṣkrodhā krodhaśamanī nirlobhā lobhanāśinī ।

niḥsaṃśayā saṃśayaghnī nirbhavā bhavanāśinī ॥ 48 ॥

Meaning

Free from anger and greed, She calms anger and destroys greed and free from doubt, She removes doubt and liberates beings from worldly becoming.

निर्विकल्पा निराबाधा निर्भेदा भेदनाशिनी ।

निर्नाशा मृत्युमथनी निष्क्रिया निष्परिग्रहा ॥ ४९॥

Pronunciation

nirvikalpā nirābādhā nirbhedā bhedanāśinī ।

nirnāśā mṛtyumathanī niṣkriyā niṣparigrahā ॥ 49 ॥

Meaning

Beyond thought constructs and all afflictions, She destroys division and being imperishable, She conquers death, acts without action and possesses nothing.

निस्तुला नीलचिकुरा निरपाया निरत्यया ।

दुर्लभा दुर्गमा दुर्गा दुःखहन्त्री सुखप्रदा ॥ ५०॥

Pronunciation

nistulā nīlacikurā nirapāyā
niratyayā ।

durlabhā durgamā durgā
duḥkhahantrī sukhapradā ॥ 50 ॥

Meaning

Incomparable and dark-haired, She is beyond decay and decline and Difficult to attain, yet the protecting Durga, She destroys sorrow and grants happiness.

दुष्टदूरा दुराचार-शमनी दोषवर्जिता ।

सर्वज्ञा सान्द्रकरुणा समानाधिक-वर्जिता ॥ ५१॥

Pronunciation

duṣṭadūrā durācāra-śamanī
doṣavarjitā ।

sarvajñā sāndrakaruṇā
samānādhika-varjitā ॥ 51 ॥

Meaning

She keeps far from the wicked, pacifies evil conduct, and is free from all defects. Omniscient and overflowing with compassion, she has none equal or superior to herself.

सर्वशक्तिमयी सर्व-मङ्गला सद्गतिप्रदा ।

सर्वेश्वरी सर्वमयी सर्वमन्त्र-स्वरूपिणी ॥ ५२॥

Pronunciation

sarvaśaktimayī sarva-maṅgalā sadgatipradā ।

sarveśvarī sarvamayī sarvamantra-svarūpiṇī ॥ 52 ॥

Meaning

She is the embodiment of all powers, all-auspicious, and the giver of the highest state. Supreme Lady of all, she pervades everything and is the essence of all mantras.

सर्व-यन्त्रात्मिका सर्व-तन्त्ररूपा मनोन्मनी ।

माहेश्वरी महादेवी महालक्ष्मीर्मृडप्रिया ॥ ५३॥

Pronunciation

sarva-yantrātmikā sarva-tantrarūpā manonmanī ।

māheśvarī mahādevī mahālakṣmīr mṛḍapriyā ॥ 53 ॥

Meaning

She is the soul of all yantras and the form of all tantras. Transcending the mind, is the Great Goddess, Mahalakshmi, and beloved of Shiva.

महारूपा महापूज्या महापातक-नाशिनी ।

महामाया महासत्त्वा महाशक्तिर्महारतिः ॥ ५४॥

Pronunciation

mahārūpā mahāpūjyā mahāpātaka-nāśinī ।

mahāmāyā mahāsattvā mahāśaktir mahāratiḥ ॥ 54 ॥

Meaning

She possesses the supreme form, is greatly worshipped and destroys even the gravest sins. She is the Great Maya, supreme essence, supreme power and the supreme delight.

महाभोगा महैश्वर्या महावीर्या महाबला ।

महाबुद्धिर्महासिद्धिर्महायोगेश्वरेश्वरी ॥ ५५॥

Pronunciation

mahābhogā mahaiśvaryā
mahāvīryā mahābalā ।

mahābuddhir mahāsiddhir
mahāyogeśvareśvarī ॥ 55 ॥

Meaning

She is supreme enjoyment, sovereignty, heroism, and strength and She is supreme wisdom, supreme accomplishment, and the Goddess of the greatest yogic lords.

महातन्त्रा महामन्त्रा महायन्त्रा महासना ।

महायाग-क्रमाराध्या महाभैरव-पूजिता ॥ ५६॥

Pronunciation

mahātantrā mahāmantrā
mahāyantrā mahāsanā ।

mahāyāga-kramārādhyā
mahābhairava-pūjitā ॥ 56 ॥

Meaning

She is the Great Tantra, Great Mantra, Great Yantra and the Supreme Seat. She is worshipped through the great sacrificial rites and adored by Mahabhairava.

महेश्वर-महाकल्प-महाताण्डव-साक्षिणी ।

महाकामेश-महिषी महात्रिपुर-सुन्दरी ॥ ५७॥

Pronunciation

maheśvara-mahākalpa-
mahātāṇḍava-sākṣiṇī ।

mahākāmeśa-mahiṣī mahātripura-
sundarī ॥ 57 ॥

Meaning

She witnesses the great cosmic dance at the end of creation and She is the Queen of Mahakamesha and the Great Beauty of the Three Worlds.

चतुःषष्ट्युपचाराढ्या चतुःषष्टिकलामयी ।

महाचतुः-षष्टिकोटि-योगिनी-गणसेविता ॥ ५८॥

Pronunciation

catuḥṣaṣṭyupacārāḍhyā catuḥṣaṣṭi-kalāmayī ।

mahācatuḥṣaṣṭi-koṭi-yoginī-gaṇa-sevitā ॥ 58 ॥

Meaning

She is worshipped with sixty four sacred offerings, embodies the sixty four arts and is served by sixty four crore Yoginis.

मनुविद्या चन्द्रविद्या चन्द्रमण्डल-मध्यगा ।

चारुरूपा चारुहासा चारुचन्द्र-कलाधरा ॥ ५९॥

Pronunciation

manuvidyā candravidyā
candramaṇḍala-madhyagā ।

cārurūpā cāruhāsā cārucandra-
kalādharā ॥ 59 ॥

Meaning

She is Manu-vidya and Candra-vidya, dwelling in the lunar sphere and beautiful in form and smile, she bears the lovely crescent moon.

चराचर-जगन्नाथा चक्रराज-निकेतना ।

पार्वती पद्मनयना पद्मराग-समप्रभा ॥ ६०॥

Pronunciation

carācara-jagannāthā cakrarāja-niketanā ।

pārvatī padmanayanā padmarāga-samaprabhā ॥ 60 ॥

Meaning

She is the Mistress of all moving and unmoving beings, residing in the Sricakra. She is Parvati, lotus-eyed and radiant like a ruby.

पञ्च-प्रेतासनासीना पञ्चब्रह्म-स्वरूपिणी ।

चिन्मयी परमानन्दा विज्ञान-घनरूपिणी ॥ ६१॥

Pronunciation

pañca-pretāsanāsīnā pañcabrahma-svarūpiṇī ।

cinmayī paramānandā vijñāna-ghana-rūpiṇī ॥ 61 ॥

Meaning

She sits upon the throne formed by the five deities and is their essential reality as pure consciousness, supreme bliss and condensed wisdom are her nature.

ध्यान-ध्यातृ-ध्येयरूपा धर्माधर्म-विवर्जिता ।

विश्वरूपा जागरिणी स्वपन्ती तैजसात्मिका ॥ ६२॥

Pronunciation

dhyāna-dhyātṛ-dhyeyarūpā
dharmādharma-vivarjitā ।

viśvarūpā jāgariṇī svapantī
taijasātmikā ॥ 62 ॥

Meaning

She is meditation, meditator, and object of meditation. Beyond virtue and vice, she is the cosmic form, present in waking and dream states.

सुप्ता प्राज्ञात्मिका तुर्या सर्वावस्था-विवर्जिता ।
सृष्टिकर्त्री ब्रह्मरूपा गोप्त्री गोविन्दरूपिणी ॥ ६३॥

Pronunciation

suptā prājñātmikā turyā
sarvāvasthā-vivarjitā ।

sṛṣṭikartrī brahmarūpā goptrī
govindarūpiṇī ॥ 63 ॥

Meaning

She abides as deep sleep, as the state of pure awareness, and as Turiya beyond all states. As Brahma, she creates, and as Govinda she preserves.

संहारिणी रुद्ररूपा तिरोधान-करीश्वरी ।

सदाशिवाऽनुग्रहदा पञ्चकृत्य-परायणा ॥ ६४॥

Pronunciation

saṃhāriṇī rudrarūpā tirodhāna-karīśvarī ।

sadāśivānugrahadā pañcakṛtya-parāyaṇā ॥ 64 ॥

Meaning

She dissolves the universe as Rudra, veils it through her power, and grants grace as Sadashiva. She is devoted to the five cosmic functions.

भानुमण्डल-मध्यस्था भैरवी भगमालिनी ।

पद्मासना भगवती पद्मनाभ-सहोदरी ॥ ६५॥

Pronunciation

bhānumaṇḍala-madhyasthā
bhairavī bhagamālinī ।

padmāsanā bhagavatī padmanābha-
sahodarī ॥ 65 ॥

Meaning

She dwells in the solar orb, is Bhairavi and Bhagamalini. Seated upon the lotus, she is the Divine Mother and sister of Padmanabha.

उन्मेष-निमिषोत्पन्न-विपन्न-भुवनावली ।

सहस्र-शीर्षवदना सहस्राक्षी सहस्रपात् ॥ ६६॥

Pronunciation

unmeṣa-nimiṣotpanna-vipanna-bhuvanāvalī ।

sahasra-śīrṣa-vadanā sahasrākṣī sahasrapāt ॥ 66 ॥

Meaning

With the opening and closing of her eyes, countless worlds arise and disappear. She has a thousand heads, faces, eyes and feet.

आब्रह्म-कीट-जननी वर्णाश्रम-विधायिनी ।

निजाज्ञारूप-निगमा पुण्यापुण्य-फलप्रदा ॥ ६७॥

Pronunciation

ābrahma-kīṭa-jananī varṇāśrama-vidhāyinī ।

nijājñārūpa-nigamā puṇyāpuṇya-phalapradā ॥ 67 ॥

Meaning

She is the mother of all beings, from Brahma to the smallest insect and the Vedas are Her command, and She dispenses the fruits of merit and demerit.

श्रुति-सीमन्त-सिन्दूरी-कृत-पादाब्ज-धूलिका ।

सकलागम-सन्दोह-शुक्ति-सम्पुट-मौक्तिका ॥ ६८॥

Pronunciation

śruti-sīmanta-sindūrī-kṛta-pādābja-dhūlikā ।

sakalāgama-sandoha-śukti-sampuṭa-mauktikā ॥ 68 ॥

Meaning

The dust of her lotus feet adorns the parting of the Vedas like vermilion. She is the pearl enclosed within the shell of all scriptures and traditions.

पुरुषार्थप्रदा पूर्णा भोगिनी भुवनेश्वरी ।

अम्बिकाऽनादि-निधना हरिब्रह्मेन्द्र-सेविता ॥ ६९॥

Pronunciation

puruṣārthapradā pūrṇā bhoginī bhuvaneśvarī ।

ambikānādi-nidhanā haribrahmendra-sevitā ॥ 69 ॥

Meaning

She grants the four aims of life and is complete in herself. The eternal Mother of the universe, she is worshipped by Vishu, Brahma and Indra.

नारायणी नादरूपा नामरूप-विवर्जिता ।

ह्रींकारी ह्रीमती हृद्या हेयोपादेय-वर्जिता ॥ ७०॥

Pronunciation

nārāyaṇī nādarūpā nāmarūpa-vivarjitā ।

hrīṃkārī hrīmatī hṛdyā heyopādeya-varjitā ॥ 70 ॥

Meaning

She is Narayani, the form of primordial sound, yet beyond all names and forms. Embodied in the mantra Hrim, she is delightful and beyond acceptance or rejection.

राजराजार्चिता राज्ञी रम्या राजीवलोचना ।

रञ्जनी रमणी रस्या रणत्किङ्किणि-मेखला ॥ ७१॥

Pronunciation

rājarājārcitā rājñī ramyā
rājīvalocanā ।

rañjanī ramaṇī rasyā raṇatkiṅkiṇi-
mekhalā ॥ 71 ॥

Meaning

Worshipped by kings of kings, she is the sovereign Queen. Lotus-eyed, charming, delightful, and adorned with a tinkling girdle.

रमा राकेन्दुवदना रतिरूपा रतिप्रिया ।
रक्षाकरी राक्षसघ्नी रामा रमणलम्पटा ॥ ७२॥

Pronunciation

ramā rākenduvadanā ratirūpā ratipriyā ।

rakṣākarī rākṣasaghnī rāmā ramaṇalampaṭā ॥ 72 ॥

Meaning

She is Lakṣmī, moon-faced, the embodiment of love and delight and She grants protection, destroys demons and rejoices in divine union.

काम्या कामकलारूपा कदम्ब-कुसुम-प्रिया ।

कल्याणी जगतीकन्दा करुणा-रस-सागरा ॥ ७३॥

Pronunciation

kāmyā kāmakalārūpā kadamba-kusuma-priyā ।

kalyāṇī jagatīkandā karuṇā-rasa-sāgarā ॥ 73 ॥

Meaning

She is desired by all, the embodiment of Kamakala, and fond of Kadamba blossoms. Auspicious and the root of the universe, she is an ocean of compassion.

कलावती कलालापा कान्ता कादम्बरीप्रिया ।

वरदा वामनयना वारुणी-मद-विह्वला ॥ ७४॥

Pronunciation

kalāvatī kalālāpā kāntā kādambarīpriyā ।

varadā vāmanayanā vāruṇī-mada-vihvalā ॥ 74 ॥

Meaning

She is endowed with every art and speaks gracefully. Beautiful and boon giving, she delights in divine bliss symbolised by the nectar of Varuni.

विश्वाधिका वेदवेद्या विन्ध्याचल-निवासिनी ।

विधात्री वेदजननी विष्णुमाया विलासिनी ॥ ७५॥

Pronunciation

viśvādhikā vedavedyā vindhyācala-nivāsinī ।

vidhātrī vedajananī viṣṇumāyā vilāsinī ॥ 75 ॥

Meaning

She transcends the universe, is known through the Vedas and dwells in the Vindhya mountains. She is the Creatrix, Mother of the Vedas and the playful power of Vishnu.

क्षेत्रस्वरूपा क्षेत्रेशी क्षेत्र-क्षेत्रज्ञ-पालिनी ।

क्षयवृद्धि-विनिर्मुक्ता क्षेत्रपाल-समर्चिता ॥ ७६॥

Pronunciation

kṣetrasvarūpā kṣetreśī kṣetra-kṣetrajña-pālinī ।

kṣayavṛddhi-vinirmuktā kṣetrapāla-samarcitā ॥ 76 ॥

Meaning

She is the very nature of the sacred field, its sovereign ruler and the protector of both the field and its knower. Beyond increase and decrease, she is worshipped by the guardians of holy places.

विजया विमला वन्द्या वन्दारु-जन-वत्सला ।

वाग्वादिनी वामकेशी वह्निमण्डल-वासिनी ॥ ७७॥

Pronunciation

vijayā vimalā vandyā vandāru-jana-vatsalā ।

vāgvādinī vāmakeśī vahnimaṇḍala-vāsinī ॥ 77 ॥

Meaning

She is victorious, pure, worthy of worship, and affectionate towards her devotees. Mistress of speech, and beautiful haired, she dwells within the circle of sacred fire.

भक्तिमत्-कल्पलतिका पशुपाश-विमोचिनी ।

संहृताशेष-पाषण्डा सदाचार-प्रवर्तिका ॥ ७८॥

Pronunciation

bhaktimat-kalpalatikā paśupāśa-vimocinī ।

saṃhṛtāśeṣa-pāṣaṇḍā sadācāra-pravartikā ॥ 78 ॥

Meaning

She is the wish fulfilling vine for devotees and liberates beings from the bonds of worldly limitation. She removes false doctrines and establishes righteous conduct.

तापत्रयाग्नि-सन्तप्त-समाह्लादन-चन्द्रिका ।

तरुणी तापसाराध्या तनुमध्या तमोऽपहा ॥ ७९॥

Pronunciation

tāpatrayāgni-santapta-
samāhlādana-candrikā ।

taruṇī tāpasārādhyā tanumadhyā
tamo'pahā ॥ 79 ॥

Meaning

She is the cooling moonlight that refreshes those scorched by the threefold sufferings. Ever youthful, worshipped by ascetics and slender waisted, she dispels all darkness.

चितिस्तत्पद-लक्ष्यार्था चिदेकरस-रूपिणी ।

स्वात्मानन्द-लवीभूत-ब्रह्माद्यानन्द-सन्ततिः ॥ ८०॥

Pronunciation

citistatpada-lakṣyārthā cidekarasa-rūpiṇī ।

svātmānanda-lavībhūta-brahmādyānanda-santatiḥ ॥ 80 ॥

Meaning

She is Pure Consciousness, the true import of the supreme Reality, and the essence of undivided awareness. The bliss of Brahma and all beings is but a tiny fraction of her own bliss.

परा प्रत्यक्चितीरूपा पश्यन्ती परदेवता ।

मध्यमा वैखरीरूपा भक्त-मानस-हंसिका ॥ ८१॥

Pronunciation

parā pratyakcitīrūpā paśyantī paradevatā ।

madhyamā vaikharīrūpā bhakta-mānasa-haṃsikā ॥ 81 ॥

Meaning

She is the supreme inward consciousness, the transcendent Goddess, and the subtle stages of speech known as Pasyanti, Madhyama, and Vaikhari. She dwells like a swan in the minds of devotees.

कामेश्वर-प्राणनाडी कृतज्ञा कामपूजिता ।

शृङ्गार-रस-सम्पूर्णा जया जालन्धर-स्थिता ॥ ८२॥

Pronunciation

kāmeśvara-prāṇanāḍī kṛtajñā kāmapūjitā ।

śṛṅgāra-rasa-sampūrṇā jayā jālandhara-sthitā ॥ 82 ॥

Meaning

She is the vital channel of Kameshvara, grateful to her devotees and worshipped through love. Filled with the essence of divine beauty and love, she abides in the sacred Jalandhara pitha.

ओड्याणपीठ-निलया बिन्दु-मण्डलवासिनी ।

रहोयाग-क्रमाराध्या रहस्तर्पण-तर्पिता ॥ ८३॥

Pronunciation

oḍyāṇapīṭha-nilayā bindu-maṇḍala-vāsinī ।

rahoyāga-kramārādhyā rahastarpaṇa-tarpitā ॥ 83 ॥

Meaning

She resides in the Odyana sacred seat and dwells in the bindu of the Sricakra and She is worshipped through secret rites and pleased by hidden offerings.

सद्यःप्रसादिनी विश्व-साक्षिणी साक्षिवर्जिता ।

षडङ्गदेवता-युक्ता षाड्गुण्य-परिपूरिता ॥ ८४॥

Pronunciation

sadyaḥprasādinī viśva-sākṣiṇī sākṣivarjitā ।

ṣaḍaṅgadevatā-yuktā ṣāḍguṇya-paripūritā ॥ 84 ॥

Meaning

She grants grace instantly, witnesses the entire universe, yet transcends even the role of witness. Accompanied by the six limb-deities, she is complete in all divine excellences.

नित्यक्लिन्ना निरुपमा निर्वाण-सुख-दायिनी ।

नित्या-षोडशिका-रूपा श्रीकण्ठार्ध-शरीरिणी ॥ ८५॥

Pronunciation

nityaklinnā nirupamā nirvāṇa-sukha-dāyinī ।

nityā-ṣoḍaśikā-rūpā śrīkaṇṭhārdha-śarīriṇī ॥ 85 ॥

Meaning

Ever softened by compassion, incomparable and bestower of liberation-bliss, she appears as the eternal sixteen fold Goddess and shares the body of Shiva.

प्रभावती प्रभारूपा प्रसिद्धा परमेश्वरी ।

मूलप्रकृतिरव्यक्ता व्यक्ताव्यक्त-स्वरूपिणी ॥
८६॥

Pronunciation

prabhāvatī prabhārūpā prasiddhā parameśvarī ।

mūlaprakṛtiravyaktā vyaktāvyakta-svarūpiṇī ॥ 86 ॥

Meaning

She is radiant and the very form of light, renowned as the Supreme Goddess, she is the primordial unmanifest nature and also the source of both the manifest and unmanifest.

व्यापिनी विविधाकारा विद्याविद्या-स्वरूपिणी ।

महाकामेश-नयन-कुमुदाह्लाद-कौमुदी ॥ ८७॥

Pronunciation

vyāpinī vividhākārā vidyāvidyā-svarūpiṇī ।

mahākāmeśa-nayana-kumudāhlāda-kaumudī ॥ 87 ॥

Meaning

She pervades all things, assumes countless forms and is both knowledge and ignorance. Like moonlight delighting lilies, she brings joy to the eyes of Mahakamesha.

भक्त-हार्द-तमोभेद-भानुमद्भानु-सन्ततिः ।

शिवदूती शिवाराध्या शिवमूर्तिः शिवङ्करी ॥ ८८॥

Pronunciation

bhakta-hārda-tamobheda-
bhānumadbhānu-santatiḥ ।

śivadūtī śivārādhyā śivamūrtiḥ
śivaṅkarī ॥ 88 ॥

Meaning

She is a succession of radiant suns dispelling the darkness in devotees' hearts. Messenger and object of worship of Shiva, she is the embodiment and bestower of auspiciousness.

शिवप्रिया शिवपरा शिष्टेष्टा शिष्टपूजिता ।

अप्रमेया स्वप्रकाशा मनोवाचामगोचरा ॥ ८९॥

Pronunciation

śivapriyā śivaparā śiṣṭeṣṭā
śiṣṭapūjitā ।

aprameyā svaprakāśā manovācām-
agocarā ॥ 89 ॥

Meaning

Beloved of Shiva and wholly devoted to him, she is cherished and worshipped by the noble. Immeasurable and self-luminous, she lies beyond mind and speech.

चिच्छक्तिश् चेतनारूपा जडशक्तिर्जडात्मिका ।

गायत्री व्याहृतिः सन्ध्या द्विजवृन्द-निषेविता ॥ ९०॥

Pronunciation

cicchaktiś cetanārūpā jaḍaśaktir jaḍātmikā ।

gāyatrī vyāhṛtiḥ sandhyā dvijavṛnda-niṣevitā ॥ 90 ॥

Meaning

She is the power of consciousness and the essence of awareness, yet also the power underlying inert matter. She is Gayatri, the sacred utterances, the twilight worship and is revered by the twice born.

तत्त्वासना तत्त्वमयी पञ्च-कोशान्तर-स्थिता ।

निःसीम-महिमा नित्य-यौवना मदशालिनी ॥ ९१॥

Pronunciation

tattvāsanā tattvamayī pañca-
kośāntara-sthitā ।

niḥsīma-mahimā nitya-yauvanā
madaśālinī ॥ 91 ॥

Meaning

She is seated upon the principles of reality and is their very essence. Dwelling within the five sheaths, her glory is limitless and she remains eternally youthful.

मदघूर्णित-रक्ताक्षी मदपाटल-गण्डभूः ।
चन्दन-द्रव-दिग्धाङ्गी चाम्पेय-कुसुम-प्रिया ॥ ९२॥

Pronunciation

madaghūrṇita-raktākṣī madapāṭala-gaṇḍabhūḥ ।

candana-drava-digdhāṅgī cāmpeya-kusuma-priyā ॥ 92 ॥

Meaning

With eyes reddened by divine ecstasy and cheeks flushed with bliss, her limbs are anointed with sandal paste and She delights in champaka flowers.

कुशला कोमलाकारा कुरुकुल्ला कुलेश्वरी ।

कुलकुण्डालया कौल-मार्ग-तत्पर-सेविता ॥ ९३॥

Pronunciation

kuśalā komalākārā kurukullā kuleśvarī ।

kulakuṇḍālayā kaula-mārga-tatpara-sevitā ॥ 93 ॥

Meaning

She is skilful, graceful, Kurukulla, and the Mistress of the Kula tradition. Dwelling in the Kula-kunda, she is served by those devoted to the Kaula path.

कुमार-गणनाथाम्बा तुष्टिः पुष्टिर्मतिर्धृतिः ।

शान्तिः स्वस्तिमती कान्तिर्नन्दिनी विघ्ननाशिनी ॥

९४॥

Pronunciation

kumāra-gaṇanāthāmbā tuṣṭiḥ puṣṭir matir dhṛtiḥ ।

śāntiḥ svastimatī kāntir nandinī vighnanāśinī ॥ 94 ॥

Meaning

She is the mother of Kumara and Ganesha. Contentment, nourishment, steadfastness, wisdom, peace, auspiciousness, beauty, joy and remover of obstacles are her forms.

तेजोवती त्रिनयना लोलाक्षी-कामरूपिणी ।

मालिनी हंसिनी माता मलयाचल-वासिनी ॥ ९५॥

Pronunciation

tejovatī trinayanā lolākṣī-
kāmarūpiṇī ।

mālinī haṃsinī mātā malayācala-
vāsinī ॥ 95 ॥

Meaning

Radiant and three eyed, with playful eyes and the form of desire itself, she is Malini, the Swan-Goddess, the Universal Mother dwelling in the Malaya mountains.

सुमुखी नलिनी सुभ्रूः शोभना सुरनायिका ।

कालकण्ठी कान्तिमती क्षोभिणी सूक्ष्मरूपिणी ॥ ९६॥

Pronunciation

sumukhī nalinī subhrūḥ śobhanā surаnāyikā ।

kālakaṇṭhī kāntimatī kṣobhiṇī sūkṣmarūpiṇī ॥ 96 ॥

Meaning

Beautiful-faced, lotus-like, with lovely brows, she is the leader of the gods. Resplendent and subtle, she stirs the universe into activity.

वज्रेश्वरी वामदेवी वयोऽवस्था-विवर्जिता ।

सिद्धेश्वरी सिद्धविद्या सिद्धमाता यशस्विनी ॥ ९७॥

Pronunciation

vajreśvarī vāmadevī vayo'vasthā-vivarjitā ।

siddheśvarī siddhavidyā siddhamātā yaśasvinī ॥ 97 ॥

Meaning

She is Vajresvari and Vamadevi, beyond all stages of age. Mistress of Siddhas, embodiment of perfected knowledge, mother of adepts and glorious.

विशुद्धिचक्र-निलयाऽऽरक्तवर्णा त्रिलोचना ।

खट्वाङ्गादि-प्रहरणा वदनैक-समन्विता ॥ ९८॥

Pronunciation

viśuddhicakra-nilayā'raktavarṇā trilocanā ।

khaṭvāṅgādi-praharaṇā vadaneka-samanvitā ॥ 98 ॥

Meaning

She resides in the Vishuddha Chakra, is reddish in hue, and three-eyed. Bearing weapons such as the khatvanga, she appears with a single face.

पायसान्नप्रिया त्वक्स्था पशुलोक-भयङ्करी ।

अमृतादि-महाशक्ति-संवृता डाकिनीश्वरी ॥ ९९॥

Pronunciation

pāyāsānnapriyā tvaksthā paśuloka-bhayaṅkarī ।

amṛtādi-mahāśakti-saṃvṛtā ḍākinīśvarī ॥ 99 ॥

Meaning

Fond of sweet milk-rice offerings and abiding in the skin element, she is fearsome to the spiritually bound. Surrounded by great powers such as Amrta, she is Dakinisvari.

अनाहताब्ज-निलया श्यामाभा वदनद्वया ।

दंष्ट्रोज्ज्वलाऽक्ष-मालादि-धरा रुधिरसंस्थिता ॥

१००॥

Pronunciation

anāhatābja-nilayā śyāmābhā vadanadvayā ।

daṃṣṭrojjvalākṣa-mālādi-dharā rudhirasaṃsthitā ॥ 100 ॥

Meaning

She resides in the lotus of the Anahata Chakra, dark hued and two faced. Bearing a rosary and other emblems with shining fangs, she abides in the principle of blood.

कालरात्र्यादि-शक्त्यौघ-वृता स्निग्धौदनप्रिया ।

महावीरेन्द्र-वरदा राकिण्यम्बा-स्वरूपिणी ॥ १०१॥

Pronunciation

kālarātryādi-śaktyaugha-vṛtā snigdhaudana-priyā ।

mahāvīrendra-varadā rākiṇyambā-svarūpiṇī ॥ 101 ॥

Meaning

She is surrounded by hosts of powers such as Kalaratri, delights in unctuous cooked rice offerings, grants boons to great heroic adepts, and manifests as Rakini Amba.

मणिपूराब्ज-निलया वदनत्रय-संयुता ।

वज्रादिकायुधोपेता डामर्यादिभिरावृता ॥ १०२॥

Pronunciation

maṇipūrābja-nilayā vadanatraya-saṃyutā ।

vajrādikāyudhopetā ḍāmaryādibhirāvṛtā ॥ 102 ॥

Meaning

She resides in the Maṇipura lotus, possesses three faces, is equipped with weapons such as the thunderbolt, and is surrounded by powers headed by Damari.

रक्तवर्णा मांसनिष्ठा गुडान्न-प्रीत-मानसा ।

समस्तभक्त-सुखदा लाकिन्यम्बा-स्वरुपिणी ॥

१०३॥

Pronunciation

raktavarṇā māṃsaniṣṭhā guḍānna-prīta-mānasā ।

samastabhakta-sukhadā lākinyambā-svarūpiṇī ॥ 103 ॥

Meaning

She is red in complexion, established in the flesh element, delights in sweet jaggery-rice offerings, bestows happiness upon all devotees and manifests as Lakini Amba.

स्वाधिष्ठानाम्बुज-गता चतुर्वक्त्र-मनोहरा ।

शूलाद्यायुध-सम्पन्ना पीतवर्णाऽतिगर्विता ॥ १०४॥

Pronunciation

svādhiṣṭhānāmbuja-gatā
caturvaktra-manoharā ।

śūlādyāyudha-sampannā
pītavarṇātigarvitā ॥ 104 ॥

Meaning

She abides in the Svadhisthana lotus, is charming with four faces, is armed with weapons beginning with the trident and shines with a radiant yellow hue.

मेदोनिष्ठा मधुप्रीता बन्धिन्यादि-समन्विता ।

दध्यन्नासक्त-हृदया काकिनी-रूप-धारिणी ॥

१०५॥

Pronunciation

medoniṣṭhā madhuprītā
bandhinyādi-samanvitā ।

dadhyannāsakta-hṛdayā kākinī-
rūpa-dhāriṇī ॥ 105 ॥

Meaning

She is established in the fatty tissue, delights in honey, is accompanied by powers such as Bandhini, is fond of curd-rice offerings and assumes the form of Kakini.

मूलाधाराम्बुजारूढा पञ्च-वक्त्राऽस्थि-संस्थिता ।

अङ्कुशादि-प्रहरणा वरदादि-निषेविता ॥ १०६॥

Pronunciation

mūlādhārāmbujārūḍhā pañca-vaktrā'sthi-saṃsthitā ।

aṅkuśādi-praharaṇā varadādi-niṣevitā ॥ 106 ॥

Meaning

She is enthroned upon the Muladhara lotus, possesses five faces, abides in the bone element, bears weapons such as the elephant-goad and is attended by boon-bestowing powers.

मुद्गौदनासक्त-चित्ता साकिन्यम्बा-स्वरूपिणी ।
आज्ञा-चक्राब्ज-निलया शुक्लवर्णा षडानना ॥
१०७॥

Pronunciation

mudgaudanāsakta-cittā
sākinyambā-svarūpiṇī ।

ājñā-cakrābja-nilayā śuklavarṇā
ṣaḍānanā ॥ 107 ॥

Meaning

She delights in offerings of mung-bean rice, manifests as Sakini Amba, resides in the lotus of the Ajna Chakra, is white in complexion and possesses six faces.

मज्जासंस्था हंसवती-मुख्य-शक्ति-समन्विता ।

हरिद्रान्नैक-रसिका हाकिनी-रूप-धारिणी ॥ १०८॥

Pronunciation

majjāsaṃsthā haṃsavatī-mukhya-śakti-samanvitā ।

haridrānnaika-rasikā hākinī-rūpa-dhāriṇī ॥ 108 ॥

Meaning

She abides in the marrow, is accompanied by principal powers such as Hamsavati, delights in turmeric-seasoned rice, and assumes the form of Hakini.

सहस्रदल-पद्मस्था सर्व-वर्णोप-शोभिता ।

सर्वायुधधरा शुक्ल-संस्थिता सर्वतोमुखी ॥ १०९॥

Pronunciation

sahasradala-padmasthā sarva-varṇopa-śobhitā ।

sarvāyudhadharā śukla-saṃsthitā sarvatomukhī ॥ 109 ॥

Meaning

She dwells in the thousand-petalled lotus, is adorned by all colours, bears every weapon, abides in pure whiteness and faces in all directions.

सर्वौदन-प्रीतचित्ता याकिन्यम्बा-स्वरूपिणी ।

स्वाहा स्वधाऽमतिर्मेधा श्रुतिः स्मृतिरनुत्तमा ॥ ११० ॥

Pronunciation

sarvaudana-prīta-cittā yākinyambā-svarūpiṇī ।

svāhā svadhā'matir medhā śrutiḥ smṛtir anuttamā ॥ 110 ॥

Meaning

She delights in all forms of food offerings, manifests as Yakini Amba, and is the essence of Svaha, Svadha, intelligence, wisdom, sacred revelation, memory, and supreme knowledge.

पुण्यकीर्तिः पुण्यलभ्या पुण्यश्रवण-कीर्तना ।

पुलोमजार्चिता बन्ध-मोचनी बन्धुरालका ॥ १११॥

Pronunciation

puṇyakīrtiḥ puṇyalabhyā
puṇyaśravaṇa-kīrtanā ।

pulomajārcitā bandha-mocanī
bandhuralakā ॥ 111 ॥

Meaning

Her fame is holy, she is attained through merit, hearing or singing her praises brings merit. Worshipped by Pulomaja (Aaci), she liberates from bondage and possesses beautiful curling locks.

विमर्शरूपिणी विद्या वियदादि-जगत्प्रसूः ।

सर्वव्याधि-प्रशमनी सर्वमृत्यु-निवारिणी ॥ ११२॥

Pronunciation

vimarśarūpiṇī vidyā viyadādi-jagatprasūḥ ।

sarvavyādhi-praśamanī sarvamṛtyu-nivāriṇī ॥ 112 ॥

Meaning

She is the embodiment of reflective consciousness (Vimarsa), true knowledge, the source of the universe beginning with space, the pacifier of all diseases, and the averter of all forms of death.

अग्रगण्याऽचिन्त्यरूपा कलिकल्मष-नाशिनी ।

कात्यायनी कालहन्त्री कमलाक्ष-निषेविता ॥ ११३॥

Pronunciation

agragaṇyā'cintyarūpā kalikalmaṣa-nāśinī ।

kātyāyanī kālahantrī kamalākṣa-niṣevitā ॥ 113 ॥

Meaning

She is foremost among all beings, of inconceivable form, destroyer of the impurities of the Kali age, Katyayani, destroyer of Time, and worshipped by Vishnu, the lotus-eyed Lord.

ताम्बूल-पूरित-मुखी दाडिमी-कुसुम-प्रभा ।
मृगाक्षी मोहिनी मुख्या मृडानी मित्ररूपिणी ॥ ११४॥

Pronunciation

tāmbūla-pūrita-mukhī dāḍimī-kusuma-prabhā ।

mṛgākṣī mohinī mukhyā mṛḍānī mitrarūpiṇī ॥ 114 ॥

Meaning

Her mouth is reddened by betel, she shines like a pomegranate blossom, has doe-like eyes, enchants all beings, is supreme among goddesses, the consort of Shiva, and appears as a friend to devotees.

नित्यतृप्ता भक्तनिधिर्नियन्त्री निखिलेश्वरी ।

मैत्र्यादि-वासनालभ्या महाप्रलय-साक्षिणी ॥ ११५॥

Pronunciation

nityatṛptā bhaktanidhir niyantrī nikhileśvarī ।

maitryādi-vāsanālabhyā mahāpralaya-sākṣiṇī ॥ 115 ॥

Meaning

She is eternally fulfilled, the treasure of devotees, the cosmic controller, sovereign of all, attainable through virtues such as friendliness and the witness of the great dissolution.

परा शक्तिः परा निष्ठा प्रज्ञानघन-रूपिणी ।

माध्वीपानालसा मत्ता मातृका-वर्ण-रूपिणी ॥
११६॥

Pronunciation

parā śaktiḥ parā niṣṭhā
prajñānaghana-rūpiṇī ।

mādhvīpānālasā mattā mātṛkā-
varṇa-rūpiṇī ॥ 116 ॥

Meaning

She is the Supreme Power, the highest goal, the embodiment of condensed pure consciousness, blissfully intoxicated by divine nectar, and the very form of the sacred alphabet.

महाकैलास-निलया मृणाल-मृदु-दोर्लता ।

महनीया दयामूर्तिर्महासाम्राज्य-शालिनी ॥ ११७॥

Pronunciation

mahākailāsa-nilayā mṛṇāla-mṛdu-dorLata ।

mahanīyā dayāmūrtir mahāsāmrājya-śālinī ॥ 117 ॥

Meaning

She resides in the great Kailasha, has arms soft as lotus stalks, is most venerable, the embodiment of compassion and possessor of supreme sovereignty.

आत्मविद्या महाविद्या श्रीविद्या कामसेविता ।

श्री-षोडशाक्षरी-विद्या त्रिकूटा कामकोटिका ॥
१९८॥

Pronunciation

ātmavidyā mahāvidyā Srividya kāmasevitā ।

śrī-ṣoḍaśākṣarī-vidyā trikūṭā kāmakoṭikā ॥ 118 ॥

Meaning

She is the knowledge of the Self, the Great Wisdom, Srividya, worshipped by Kama, she is the sacred sixteen syllabled mantra, the three peaked mantra and the source of countless desires fulfilled.

कटाक्ष-किङ्करी-भूत-कमला-कोटि-सेविता ।

शिरःस्थिता चन्द्रनिभा भालस्थेन्द्र-धनुःप्रभा ॥ ११९॥

Pronunciation

kaṭākṣa-kiṅkarī-bhūta-kamalā-koṭi-sevitā ।

śiraḥsthitā candranibhā bhālasthendra-dhanuḥ-prabhā ॥ 119 ॥

Meaning

Millions of Lakshmis stand as attendants awaiting her glance. She shines like the moon at the crown and like a rainbow upon the forehead.

हृदयस्था रविप्रख्या त्रिकोणान्तर-दीपिका ।

दाक्षायणी दैत्यहन्त्री दक्षयज्ञ-विनाशिनी ॥ १२०॥

Pronunciation

hṛdayasthā raviprakhyā
trikoṇāntara-dīpikā ।

dākṣāyaṇī daityahantrī dakṣayajña-
vināśinī ॥ 120 ॥

Meaning

She resides in the heart, radiant like the sun, the lamp shining within the mystic triangle, she is Dakshayani, destroyer of demons and the one who brought about the destruction of Daksha's sacrifice.

दरान्दोलित-दीर्घाक्षी दर-हासोज्ज्वलन्-मुखी ।
गुरुमूर्तिर्गुणनिधिर्गोमाता गुहजन्मभूः ॥ १२१॥

Pronunciation

darāndolita-dīrghākṣī dara-hāsojjvalan-mukhī ।

gurumūrtir guṇanidhir gomātā guhajanmabhūḥ ॥ 121 ॥

Meaning

Her long eyes move gracefully, her face shines with a gentle smile. She is the embodiment of the Guru, the treasure house of virtues, the universal Mother, and the source of Skanda.

देवेशी दण्डनीतिस्था दहराकाश-रूपिणी ।

प्रतिपन्मुख्य-राकान्त-तिथि-मण्डल-पूजिता ॥

१२२॥

Pronunciation

deveśī daṇḍanītisthā daharākāśa-rūpiṇī ।

pratipanmukhya-rākānta-tithi-maṇḍala-pūjitā ॥ 122 ॥

Meaning

She is the Queen of the gods, established in cosmic order and discipline, the form of the subtle inner space of the heart and worshipped through all lunar phases from Pratipad to Pūrṇimā.

कलात्मिका कलानाथा काव्यालाप-विनोदिनी ।
सचामर-रमा-वाणी-सव्य-दक्षिण-सेविता ॥ १२३॥

Pronunciation

kalātmikā kalānāthā kāvyālāpa-vinodinī ।

sacāmara-ramā-vāṇī-savya-dakṣiṇa-sevitā ॥ 123 ॥

Meaning

She is the essence of all arts, their sovereign mistress, delighting in poetic discourse. Lakshmi and Sarasvati attend her on either side, bearing fly-whisks.

आदिशक्तिरमेयाऽऽत्मा परमा पावनाकृतिः ।

अनेककोटि-ब्रह्माण्ड-जननी दिव्यविग्रहा ॥ १२४॥

Pronunciation

ādiśaktir ameyātmā paramā
pāvanākṛtiḥ ।

anekakoṭi-brahmāṇḍa-jananī
divyavigrahā ॥ 124 ॥

Meaning

She is the Primordial Power, immeasurable in essence, supreme and purifying, the mother of countless universes and possessed of a divine form.

क्लींकारी केवला गुह्या कैवल्य-पददायिनी ।

त्रिपुरा त्रिजगद्वन्द्या त्रिमूर्तिस्त्रिदशेश्वरी ॥ १२५॥

Pronunciation

klīṃkārī kevalā guhyā kaivalya-padadāyinī ।

tripurā trijagadvandyā trimūrtis tridaśeśvarī ॥ 125 ॥

Meaning

She is embodied in the seed syllable Klim, absolute and secret, the giver of liberation, Tripura, revered in the three worlds, the essence of the Trimurti and sovereign of the gods.

त्र्यक्षरी दिव्य-गन्धाढ्या सिन्दूर-तिलकाञ्चिता ।

उमा शैलेन्द्रतनया गौरी गन्धर्व-सेविता ॥ १२६॥

Pronunciation

tryakṣarī divya-gandhāḍhyā
sindūra-tilakāñcitā ।

umā śailendratanayā gaurī
gandharva-sevitā ॥ 126 ॥

Meaning

She is the three-syllabled mantra, richly adorned with divine fragrance, beautified by vermilion upon her forehead, she is Uma, daughter of the Lord of Mountains, Gauri, and is served by the Gandharvas.

विश्वगर्भा स्वर्णगर्भाऽवरदा वागधीश्वरी ।

ध्यानगम्याऽपरिच्छेद्या ज्ञानदा ज्ञानविग्रहा ॥ १२७॥

Pronunciation

viśvagarbhā svarṇagarbhā varadā vāgadhīśvarī ।

dhyānagamyāparicchedyā jñānadā jñānavigrahā ॥ 127 ॥

Meaning

She bears the universe within herself, is the golden womb of creation, the granter of boons and sovereign of speech, attainable through meditation, immeasurable, the giver of knowledge and knowledge itself embodied.

सर्ववेदान्त-संवेद्या सत्यानन्द-स्वरूपिणी ।

लोपामुद्रार्चिता लीला-क्लृप्त-ब्रह्माण्ड-मण्डला ॥
१२८॥

Pronunciation

sarvavedānta-saṃvedyā
satyānanda-svarūpiṇī ।

lopāmudrārcitā līlā-kḷpta-
brahmāṇḍa-maṇḍalā ॥ 128 ॥

Meaning

She is realized through all Vedanta, the embodiment of Truth and Bliss, worshipped by Lopamudra, and who playfully manifests the cosmic universe.

अदृश्या दृश्यरहिता विज्ञात्री वेद्यवर्जिता ।

योगिनी योगदा योग्या योगानन्दा युगन्धरा ॥ १२९॥

Pronunciation

adṛśyā dṛśyarahitā vijñātrī vedyavarjitā ।

yoginī yogadā yogyā yogānandā yugandharā ॥ 129 ॥

Meaning

She is invisible, beyond all objects of perception, the knower beyond the known, the Yogini, giver of yoga, worthy of yoga, bliss of yoga and supporter of the ages.

इच्छाशक्ति-ज्ञानशक्ति-क्रियाशक्ति-स्वरूपिणी ।

सर्वाधारा सुप्रतिष्ठा सदसद्रूप-धारिणी ॥ १३०॥

Pronunciation

icchāśakti-jñānaśakti-kriyāśakti-svarūpiṇī ।

sarvādhārā supratiṣṭhā sadasadrūpa-dhāriṇī ॥ 130 ॥

Meaning

She is the embodiment of the powers of Will, Knowledge and Action, the support of all, firmly established and the bearer of both being and non-being.

अष्टमूर्तिरजाजैत्री लोकयात्रा-विधायिनी ।

एकाकिनी भूमरूपा निर्द्वैता द्वैतवर्जिता ॥ १३१॥

Pronunciation

aṣṭamūrtir ajājaitrī lokayātrā-
vidhāyinī ।

ekākinī bhūmarūpā nirdvaitā
dvaitavarjitā ॥ 131 ॥

Meaning

She manifests as the eight forms of Shiva, triumphs over Maya, and governs the course of the worlds, solitary, infinite, non-dual and free from all duality.

अन्नदा वसुदा वृद्धा ब्रह्मात्मैक्य-स्वरूपिणी ।

बृहती ब्राह्मणी ब्राह्मी ब्रह्मानन्दा बलिप्रिया ॥
१३२॥

Pronunciation

annadā vasudā vṛddhā
brahmātmaikya-svarūpiṇī ।

bṛhatī brāhmaṇī brāhmī
brahmānandā balipriyā ॥ 132 ॥

Meaning

She gives food and wealth, is ancient and ever-growing, embodies the unity of Brahman and Self, the Vast One, Brahmani, Brahmī, the bliss of Brahman and fond of sacred offerings.

भाषारूपा बृहत्सेना भावाभाव-विवर्जिता ।

सुखाराध्या शुभकरी शोभना सुलभा गतिः ॥ १३३॥

Pronunciation

bhāṣārūpā bṛhatsenā bhāvābhāva-vivarjitā ।

sukhārādhyā śubhakārī śobhanā sulabhā gatiḥ ॥ 133 ॥

Meaning

She is the essence of language, commander of vast hosts, beyond existence and non-existence, easily worshipped, bestower of auspiciousness, beautiful, and the readily attainable goal.

राज-राजेश्वरी राज्य-दायिनी राज्य-वल्लभा ।

राजत्कृपा राजपीठ-निवेशित-निजाश्रिता ॥ १३४॥

Pronunciation

rājarājeśvarī rājyadāyinī
rājyavallabhā ।

rājatkṛpā rājapīṭha-niveśita-
nijāśritā ॥ 134 ॥

Meaning

She is the Queen of kings, giver of sovereignty, beloved of rulers, whose radiant grace enthrones her devotees in positions of authority.

राज्यलक्ष्मीः कोशनाथा चतुरङ्ग-बलेश्वरी ।

साम्राज्य-दायिनी सत्यसन्धा सागरमेखला ॥ १३५॥

Pronunciation

rājyalakṣmīḥ kośanāthā caturaṅga-baleśvarī ।

sāmrājya-dāyinī satyasaṃdhā sāgaramekhalā ॥ 135 ॥

Meaning

She is the fortune of kingdoms, mistress of treasures, sovereign of the fourfold army, giver of empire, true to her promises and girdled by the oceans.

दीक्षिता दैत्यशमनी सर्वलोक-वशङ्करी ।

सर्वार्थदात्री सावित्री सच्चिदानन्द-रूपिणी ॥ १३६॥

Pronunciation

dīkṣitā daityaśamanī sarvaloka-vaśaṅkarī ।

sarvārthadātrī sāvitrī saccidānanda-rūpiṇī ॥ 136 ॥

Meaning

She is initiated into all sacred mysteries, subduer of demons, enchantress of all worlds, giver of every attainment, Savitri and the embodiment of Existence, Consciousness and Bliss.

देश-कालापरिच्छिन्ना सर्वगा सर्वमोहिनी ।

सरस्वती शास्त्रमयी गुहाम्बा गुह्यरूपिणी ॥ १३७॥

Pronunciation

deśa-kālāparicchinnā sarvagā sarvamohinī ।

sarasvatī śāstramayī guhāmbā guhyarūpiṇī ॥ 137 ॥

Meaning

She is unbounded by space and time, all-pervading, enchantress of all, Sarasvati, embodied in the scriptures, Mother of Guha (Skanda) and of mysterious form.

सर्वोपाधि-विनिर्मुक्ता सदाशिव-पतिव्रता ।

सम्प्रदायेश्वरी साध्वी गुरुमण्डल-रूपिणी ॥ १३८॥

Pronunciation

sarvopādhi-vinirmuktā sadāśiva-pativratā ।

sampradāyeśvarī sādhvī gurumaṇḍala-rūpiṇī ॥ 138 ॥

Meaning

She is free from all limiting adjuncts, devoted to Sadashiva, sovereign of the sacred tradition, virtuous and the embodiment of the lineage of Gurus.

कुलोत्तीर्णा भगाराध्या माया मधुमती मही ।

गणाम्बा गुह्यकाराध्या कोमलाङ्गी गुरुप्रिया ॥
१३९॥

Pronunciation

kulottīrṇā bhagārādhyā māyā
madhumatī mahī ।

gaṇāmbā guhyakārādhyā komalāṅgī
gurupriyā ॥ 139 ॥

Meaning

She transcends all spiritual clans, is worshipped through the Bhaga principle, is Maya, sweetly radiant, and the Earth itself, Mother of the hosts, adored by hidden beings, tender-limbed, and dear to the Guru.

स्वतन्त्रा सर्वतन्त्रेशी दक्षिणामूर्ति-रूपिणी ।

सनकादि-समाराध्या शिवज्ञान-प्रदायिनी ॥ १४० ॥

Pronunciation

svatantrā sarvatantrēśī dakṣiṇāmūrti-rūpiṇī ।

sanakādi-samārādhyā śivajñāna-pradāyinī ॥ 140 ॥

Meaning

She is absolutely independent, sovereign of all Tantras, manifest as Dakshinamurti, worshipped by sages such as Sanaka and bestower of the knowledge of Shiva.

चित्कलाऽऽनन्द-कलिका प्रेमरूपा प्रियङ्करी ।

नामपारायण-प्रीता नन्दिविद्या नटेश्वरी ॥ १४१॥

Pronunciation

citkalānanda-kalikā premarūpā priyaṅkarī ।

nāmapārāyaṇa-prītā nandividyā naṭeśvarī ॥ 141 ॥

Meaning

She is the bud of bliss arising from pure consciousness, the embodiment of love and giver of delight, pleased by the recitation of her names, the wisdom of Nandin and the Lady of Divine Dance.

मिथ्या-जगदधिष्ठाना मुक्तिदा मुक्तिरूपिणी ।
लास्यप्रिया लयकरी लज्जा रम्भादिवन्दिता ॥
१४२॥

Pronunciation

mithyā-jagad-adhiṣṭhānā muktidā muktirūpiṇī ।

lāsyapriyā layakarī lajjā rambhādivanditā ॥ 142 ॥

Meaning

She is the substratum of the illusory universe, giver of liberation and liberation itself, fond of graceful dance, dissolver of the cosmos, modesty incarnate and worshipped by celestial maidens such as Rambha.

भवदाव-सुधावृष्टिः पापारण्य-दवानला ।

दौर्भाग्य-तूलवातूला जराध्वान्त-रविप्रभा ॥ १४३॥

Pronunciation

bhavadāva-sudhāvṛṣṭiḥ pāpāraṇya-davānalā ।

daurbhāgya-tūlavātūlā jarādhvānta-raviprabhā ॥ 143 ॥

Meaning

She is the nectar-rain that extinguishes the forest fire of worldly existence, the wildfire that consumes the forest of sin, the gale that scatters the cotton of misfortune and the sun that dispels the darkness of old age.

भाग्याब्धि-चन्द्रिका भक्त-चित्तकेकि-घनाघना ।

रोगपर्वत-दम्भोलिर्मृत्युदारु-कुठारिका ॥ १४४॥

Pronunciation

bhāgyābdhi-candrikā bhakta-cittakeki-ghanāghanā ।

rogaparvata-dambholir mṛtyudāru-kuṭhārikā ॥ 144 ॥

Meaning

She is the moonlight upon the ocean of fortune, the raincloud that delights the peacocks of devotees' hearts, the thunderbolt that shatters the mountain of disease, and the axe that fells the tree of death.

महेश्वरी महाकाली महाग्रासा महाशना ।

अपर्णा चण्डिका चण्डमुण्डासुर-निषूदिनी ॥ १४५॥

Pronunciation

maheśvarī mahākālī mahāgrāsā mahāśanā ।

aparṇā caṇḍikā caṇḍamuṇḍāsura-niṣūdinī ॥ 145 ॥

Meaning

She is the Great Goddess, Mahakali, devourer of all, consumer of the universe, Aparna, Candika, and destroyer of the demons, Canda and Munda.

क्षराक्षरात्मिका सर्व-लोकेशी विश्वधारिणी ।

त्रिवर्गदात्री सुभगा त्र्यम्बका त्रिगुणात्मिका ॥ १४६॥

Pronunciation

kṣarākṣarātmikā sarvalokeśī viśvadhāriṇī ।

trivargadātrī subhagā tryambakā triguṇātmikā ॥ 146 ॥

Meaning

She is the essence of both the perishable and imperishable, sovereign of all worlds, supporter of the universe, giver of the three aims of life, auspicious, three-eyed and constituted of the three gunas.

स्वर्गापवर्गदा शुद्धा जपापुष्प-निभाकृतिः ।

ओजोवती द्युतिधरा यज्ञरूपा प्रियव्रता ॥ १४७॥

Pronunciation

svargāpavargadā śuddhā japāpuṣpa-nibhākṛtiḥ ।

ojovatī dyutidharā yajñarūpā priyavratā ॥ 147 ॥

Meaning

She grants both heaven and liberation, is pure and shines with the hue of the hibiscus flower, full of vigour, radiant, the embodiment of sacrifice and devoted to sacred vows.

दुराराध्या दुराधर्षा पाटली-कुसुम-प्रिया ।

महती मेरुनिलया मन्दार-कुसुम-प्रिया ॥ १४८॥

Pronunciation

durārādhyā durādharṣā pāṭalī-kusuma-priyā ।

mahatī merunilayā mandāra-kusuma-priyā ॥ 148 ॥

Meaning

She is difficult to worship and impossible to overcome, fond of patali blossoms, the Great One who dwells upon Mount Meru and delights in mandara flowers.

वीराराध्या विराड्रूपा विरजा विश्वतोमुखी ।

प्रत्यग्रूपा पराकाशा प्राणदा प्राणरूपिणी ॥ १४९॥

Pronunciation

vīrārādhyā virāḍrūpā virajā viśvatomukhī ।

pratyagrūpā parākāśā prāṇadā prāṇarūpiṇī ॥ 149 ॥

Meaning

She is worshipped by heroic adepts, possesses the cosmic Virat form, is stainless and faces all directions, her nature is the innermost Self, the supreme space, the giver of life and life itself.

मार्ताण्ड-भैरवाराध्या मन्त्रिणीन्यस्त-राज्यधूः ।

त्रिपुरेशी जयत्सेना निस्त्रैगुण्या परापरा ॥ १५०॥

Pronunciation

mārtāṇḍa-bhairavārādhyā
mantriṇīnyasta-rājyadhūḥ ।

tripureśī jayatsenā nistraiguṇyā
parāparā ॥ 150 ॥

Meaning

She is worshipped by Martanda Bhairava, has entrusted the burden of governance to her ministerial power, is the Queen of Tripura, whose armies are ever victorious, beyond the three gunas and both transcendent and immanent.

सत्य-ज्ञानानन्द-रूपा सामरस्य-परायणा ।

कपर्दिनी कलामाला कामधुक् कामरूपिणी ॥ १५१॥

Pronunciation

satya-jñānānanda-rūpā sāmarasya-parāyaṇā ।

kapardinī kalāmālā kāmadhuk kāmarūpiṇī ॥ 151 ॥

Meaning

She, whose nature is Truth, Knowledge and Bliss, who is devoted to the state of perfect spiritual harmony, the matted-haired One, garlanded with all arts and powers, the wish-fulfilling source of all desires and the embodiment of desire itself.

कलानिधिः काव्यकला रसज्ञा रसशेवधिः ।

पुष्टा पुरातना पूज्या पुष्करा पुष्करेक्षणा ॥ १५२॥

Pronunciation

kalānidhiḥ kāvyakalā rasajñā rasaśevadhiḥ ।

puṣṭā purātanā pūjyā puṣkarā puṣkarekṣaṇā ॥ 152 ॥

Meaning

She, who is the treasure house of arts, the art of poetry, the knower of all aesthetic delight, the repository of rasa, ever-nourishing, ancient, worthy of worship, lotus-like and lotus-eyed.

परंज्योतिः परंधाम परमाणुः परात्परा ।

पाशहस्ता पाशहन्त्री परमन्त्र-विभेदिनी ॥ १५३॥

Pronunciation

paraṃjyotiḥ paraṃdhāma
paramāṇuḥ parātparā ।

pāśahastā pāśahantrī paramantra-
vibhedinī ॥ 153 ॥

Meaning

She, who is the Supreme Light, the Supreme Abode, subtler than the smallest atom, transcending even the highest, holding the noose, destroyer of bondage and knower of the innermost secret of all mantras.

मूर्ताऽमूर्ताऽनित्यतृप्ता मुनिमानस-हंसिका ।
सत्यव्रता सत्यरूपा सर्वान्तर्यामिनी सती ॥ १५४॥

Pronunciation

mūrtāmūrtā nityatṛptā
munimānasa-haṃsikā ।

satyavratā satyarūpā
sarvāntaryāminī satī ॥ 154 ॥

Meaning

She, who is both with form and beyond form, eternally fulfilled, the swan dwelling in the minds of sages, devoted to truth, Truth itself, the indwelling ruler of all beings and the eternal faithful One.

ब्रह्माणी ब्रह्मजननी बहुरूपा बुधार्चिता ।

प्रसवित्री प्रचण्डाऽऽज्ञा प्रतिष्ठा प्रकटाकृतिः ॥ १५५॥

Pronunciation

brahmāṇī brahmajananī bahurūpā budhārcitā ।

prasavitri pracaṇḍājñā pratiṣṭhā prakaṭākṛtiḥ ॥ 155 ॥

Meaning

She, who is Brahmani, the Mother of Brahma, assuming many forms and worshipped by the wise, the Creatrix, whose command is irresistible, the foundation of existence and who manifests reality itself.

प्राणेश्वरी प्राणदात्री पञ्चाशत्पीठ-रूपिणी ।

विशृङ्खला विविक्तस्था वीरमाता वियत्प्रसूः ॥
१५६॥

Pronunciation

prāṇeśvarī prāṇadātrī
pañcāśatpīṭha-rūpiṇī ।

viśṛṅkhalā viviktasthā vīramātā
viyatprasūḥ ॥ 156 ॥

Meaning

She, who is the sovereign of life-force and the giver of life, embodied as the fifty sacred seats (letters), free from all limitations, established in transcendence, Mother of heroes and source of space itself.

मुकुन्दा मुक्तिनिलया मूलविग्रह-रूपिणी ।

भावज्ञा भवरोगघ्नी भवचक्र-प्रवर्तिनी ॥ १५७॥

Pronunciation

mukundā muktinilayā mūlavigraha-rūpiṇī ।

bhāvajñā bhavarogaghnī bhavacakra-pravartinī ॥ 157 ॥

Meaning

She, who grants liberation, the abode of liberation, the primordial form, knower of all inner feelings, destroyer of the disease of worldly existence and mover of the wheels of becoming.

छन्दःसारा शास्त्रसारा मन्त्रसारा तलोदरी ।

उदारकीर्तिरुद्दामवैभवा वर्णरूपिणी ॥ १५८॥

Pronunciation

chandaḥsārā śāstrasārā mantrasārā talodarī ।

udārakīrtiruddāmavaibhavā varṇarūpiṇī ॥ 158 ॥

Meaning

She, who is the essence of the Vedas, scriptures, and mantras, slender waisted, of noble fame, possessing boundless glory and manifest as all letters and sounds.

जन्ममृत्यु-जरातप्त-जनविश्रान्ति-दायिनी ।

सर्वोपनिष-दुद्-घुष्टा शान्त्यतीत-कलात्मिका ॥
१५९॥

Pronunciation

janmamṛtyu-jarātapta-janaviśrānti-dāyinī ।

sarvopaniṣadudghuṣṭā śāntyatīta-kalātmikā ॥ 159 ॥

Meaning

She, who grants rest to beings afflicted by birth, death and old age, proclaimed by all the Upanishads and whose nature transcends even the highest state of peace.

गम्भीरा गगनान्तस्था गर्विता गानलोलुपा ।

कल्पना-रहिता काष्ठाऽकान्ता कान्तार्ध-विग्रहा ॥ १६०॥

Pronunciation

gambhīrā gaganāntasthā garvitā gānalolupā ।

kalpanā-rahitā kāṣṭhākāntā kāntārdha-vigrahā ॥ 160 ॥

Meaning

She, who is profound, abiding in the limitless sky of consciousness, majestic, delighting in sacred song, beyond imagination, the supreme state and sharing half the form of her Beloved.

कार्यकारण-निर्मुक्ता कामकेलि-तरङ्गिता ।

कनत्कनकता-टङ्का लीला-विग्रह-धारिणी ॥ १६१॥

Pronunciation

kāryakāraṇa-nirmuktā kāmakeli-taraṅgitā ।

kanatkanakatāṭaṅkā līlā-vigraha-dhāriṇī ॥ 161 ॥

Meaning

She, who is free from cause and effect, yet sports in the waves of divine love, adorned with shining golden earrings and assuming forms for the sake of divine play.

अजा क्षयविनिर्मुक्ता मुग्धा क्षिप्र-प्रसादिनी ।

अन्तर्मुख-समाराध्या बहिर्मुख-सुदुर्लभा ॥ १६२॥

Pronunciation

ajā kṣayavinirmuktā mugdhā
kṣipra-prasādinī ।

antarmukha-samārādhyā
bahirmukha-sudurlabhā ॥ 162 ॥

Meaning

She, who is unborn, free from decay, enchanting, and quickly pleased, easily worshipped by the inward-turned seeker, but difficult to attain for the outward-turned mind.

त्रयी त्रिवर्गनिलया त्रिस्था त्रिपुरमालिनी ।

निरामया निरालम्बा स्वात्मारामा सुधास्रुतिः ॥ १६३॥

Pronunciation

trayī trivarganilayā tristhā tripuramālinī ।

nirāmayā nirālambā svātmārāmā sudhāsrutiḥ ॥ 163 ॥

Meaning

She, who is the threefold Veda, the abode of the three aims of life, established in the three states, and adorned as Tripuramalini, free from all affliction, self-supported, rejoicing in Her own Self, and flowing as nectar.

संसारपङ्क-निर्मग्न-समुद्धरण-पण्डिता ।

यज्ञप्रिया यज्ञकर्त्री यजमान-स्वरूपिणी ॥ १६४॥

Pronunciation

saṃsārapaṅka-nirmagna-samuddharaṇa-paṇḍitā ।

yajñapriyā yajñakartrī yajamāna-svarūpiṇī ॥ 164 ॥

Meaning

She, who is skilled in rescuing beings sunk in the mire of worldly existence, lover of sacrifice, performer of sacrifice and the very sacrificer.

धर्माधारा धनाध्यक्षा धनधान्य-विवर्धिनी ।

विप्रप्रिया विप्ररूपा विश्वभ्रमण-कारिणी ॥ १६५॥

Pronunciation

dharmādhārā dhanādhyakṣā dhanadhānya-vivardhinī ।

viprapriyā viprarūpā viśvabhramaṇa-kāriṇī ॥ 165 ॥

Meaning

She, who is the support of righteousness, overseer of wealth, increaser of prosperity and grain, dear to the wise, assuming the form of the wise, and causing the movement of the universe.

विश्वग्रासा विद्रुमाभा वैष्णवी विष्णुरूपिणी ।

अयोनिर्योनिनिलया कूटस्था कुलरूपिणी ॥ १६६॥

Pronunciation

viśvagrāsā vidrumābhā vaiṣṇavī viṣṇurūpiṇī ।

ayoniryoninilayā kūṭasthā kularūpiṇī ॥ 166 ॥

Meaning

She, who absorbs the universe into Herself, coral-hued, the power of Vishu and Vishnu Himself, unborn yet dwelling in the source of all births, immutable and the embodiment of the Kula principle.

वीरगोष्ठीप्रिया वीरा नैष्कर्म्या नादरूपिणी ।

विज्ञानकलना कल्या विदग्धा बैन्दवासना ॥ १६७॥

Pronunciation

vīragoṣṭhīpriyā vīrā naiṣkarmyā nādarūpiṇī ।

vijñānakalanā kalyā vidagdhā baindavāsanā ॥ 167 ॥

Meaning

She, who delights in the assembly of spiritual heroes, Herself heroic, beyond action, embodied as primordial sound, the source of higher wisdom, auspicious, skilful and established in the bindu.

तत्त्वाधिका तत्त्वमयी तत्त्वमर्थ-स्वरूपिणी ।

सामगानप्रिया सौम्या सदाशिव-कुटुम्बिनी ॥ १६८॥

Pronunciation

tattvādhikā tattvamayī tattvamartha-svarūpiṇī ।

sāmagānapriyā saumyā sadāśiva-kuṭumbinī ॥ 168 ॥

Meaning

She, who transcends all principles while being their very essence, the meaning of the great truth, fond of Sama-vedic chant, gentle and serene, and the consort of Sadashiva.

सव्यापसव्य-मार्गस्था सर्वापद्विनिवारिणी ।

स्वस्था स्वभावमधुरा धीरा धीरसमर्चिता ॥ १६९॥

Pronunciation

savyāpasavya-mārgasthā sarvāpad-vinivāriṇī ।

svasthā svabhāvamadhurā dhīrā dhīrasamarcitā ॥ 169 ॥

Meaning

She, who abides in both right-hand and left-hand spiritual paths, remover of all dangers, established in Her own nature, inherently sweet, steadfast, and worshipped by the wise.

चैतन्यार्घ्य-समाराध्या चैतन्य-कुसुमप्रिया ।

सदोदिता सदातुष्टा तरुणादित्य-पाटला ॥ १७०॥

Pronunciation

caitanyārghya-samārādhyā caitanya-kusumapriyā ।

sadoditā sadātuṣṭā taruṇāditya-pāṭalā ॥ 170 ॥

Meaning

She, who is worshipped with the offering of pure consciousness, who delights in the flowers of awareness, ever-risen, ever-content, and radiant like the young rising sun.

दक्षिणा-दक्षिणाराध्या दरस्मेर-मुखाम्बुजा ।

कौलिनी-केवलाऽनर्घ्य-कैवल्य-पददायिनी ॥

१७१॥

Pronunciation

dakṣiṇā-dakṣiṇārādhyā darasmera-mukhāmbujā ।

kaulinī-kevalānarghya-kaivalya-padadāyinī ॥ 171 ॥

Meaning

She, who is generosity itself and worshipped through the Dakshinacara path, whose lotus-face bears a gentle smile, the supreme Kaulini, incomparable and the bestower of liberation.

स्तोत्रप्रिया स्तुतिमती श्रुति-संस्तुत-वैभवा ।
मनस्विनी मानवती महेशी मङ्गलाकृतिः ॥ १७२॥

Pronunciation

stotrapriyā stutimatī śruti-saṃstuta-vaibhavā ।

manasvinī mānavatī maheśī maṅgalākṛtiḥ ॥ 172 ॥

Meaning

She, who delights in hymns, rich in praise, whose glory is celebrated by the Vedas, noble-minded, compassionate toward humanity, the Great Goddess and the embodiment of auspiciousness.

विश्वमाता जगद्धात्री विशालाक्षी विरागिणी ।

प्रगल्भा परमोदारा परामोदा मनोमयी ॥ १७३॥

Pronunciation

viśvamātā jagaddhātrī viśālākṣī virāgiṇī ।

pragalbhā paramodārā parāmodā manomayī ॥ 173 ॥

Meaning

She, who is the Mother of the universe, sustainer of the worlds, wide-eyed, detached, confident, supremely generous, filled with transcendent delight and pervading the mind.

व्योमकेशी विमानस्था वज्रिणी वामकेश्वरी ।

पञ्चयज्ञ-प्रिया पञ्च-प्रेत-मञ्चाधिशायिनी ॥ १७४॥

Pronunciation

vyomakeśī vimānasthā vajriṇī
vāmakeśvarī ।

pañcayajña-priyā pañca-preta-
mañcādhiśāyinī ॥ 174 ॥

Meaning

She, whose hair is the sky itself, who abides in the celestial vehicle, wielder of power, Lady of Vamakeshvara, fond of the five sacrifices and reclining upon the couch formed by the five deities.

पञ्चमी पञ्चभूतेशी पञ्च-संख्योपचारिणी ।

शाश्वती शाश्वतैश्वर्या शर्मदा शम्भुमोहिनी ॥ १७५॥

Pronunciation

pañcamī pañcabhūteśī pañca-saṃkhyopacāriṇī ।

śāśvatī śāśvataiśvaryā śarmadā śambhumohinī ॥ 175 ॥

Meaning

She, who is Pancami, sovereign of the five elements, worshipped through the fivefold offerings, eternal, possessing everlasting sovereignty, bestower of bliss, and enchantress even of Shambhu (Shiva).

धराधरसुता धन्या धर्मिणी धर्मवर्धिनी ।

लोकातीता गुणातीता सर्वातीता शमात्मिका ॥

१७६॥

Pronunciation

dharādharasutā dhanyā dharmiṇī dharmavardhinī ।

lokātītā guṇātītā sarvātītā śamātmikā ॥ 176 ॥

Meaning

She, who is the daughter of the Mountain, blessed and virtuous, who nourishes righteousness, transcending the worlds, beyond the gunas, beyond all limitations and whose nature is supreme peace.

बन्धूक-कुसुमप्रख्या बाला लीलाविनोदिनी ।

सुमङ्गली सुखकरी सुवेषाढ्या सुवासिनी ॥ १७७॥

Pronunciation

bandhūka-kusuma-prakhyā bālā līlā-vinodinī ।

sumaṅgalī sukhakarī suveṣāḍhyā suvāsinī ॥ 177 ॥

Meaning

She, who shines like the red bandhuka flower, ever youthful, delighting in divine play, auspicious, bestower of happiness, beautifully adorned and dwelling in purity and grace.

सुवासिन्यर्चन-प्रीताऽऽशोभना शुद्धमानसा ।
बिन्दु-तर्पण-सन्तुष्टा पूर्वजा त्रिपुराम्बिका ॥ १७८॥

Pronunciation

suvāsinyarcana-prītā śobhanā śuddhamānasā ।

bindu-tarpaṇa-santuṣṭā pūrvajā tripurāmbikā ॥ 178 ॥

Meaning

She, who is pleased by the worship of married women, radiant and beautiful, pure in mind, satisfied by offerings made to the sacred bindu, the Primordial One and Mother Tripura.

दशमुद्रा-समाराध्या त्रिपुराश्री-वशङ्करी ।

ज्ञानमुद्रा ज्ञानगम्या ज्ञानज्ञेय-स्वरूपिणी ॥ १७९॥

Pronunciation

daśamudrā-samārādhyā tripurāśrī-vaśaṅkarī ।

jñānamudrā jñānagamyā jñānajñeya-svarūpiṇī ॥ 179 ॥

Meaning

She, who is worshipped through the ten sacred mudras, who brings all under the grace of Tripura, the gesture of wisdom, attainable through knowledge and the very essence of knowledge and its object.

योनिमुद्रा त्रिखण्डेशी त्रिगुणाम्बा त्रिकोणगा ।

अनघाऽद्भुत-चारित्रा वाञ्छितार्थ-प्रदायिनी ॥ १८० ॥

Pronunciation

yonimudrā trikhaṇḍeśī triguṇāmbā trikoṇagā ।

anaghādbhuta-cāritrā vāñchitārtha-pradāyinī ॥ 180 ॥

Meaning

She, who is represented by the yoni-mudra, Mistress of the three sections (of Srividya), Mother of the three guṇas, abiding in the sacred triangle, sinless, of wondrous deeds, and granter of all desired attainments.

अभ्यासातिशय-ज्ञाता षडध्वातीत-रूपिणी ।

अव्याज-करुणा-मूर्तिरज्ञान-ध्वान्त-दीपिका ॥

१८१॥

Pronunciation

abhyāsātiśaya-jñātā ṣaḍadhvātīta-rūpiṇī ।

avyāja-karuṇā-mūrtirajñāna-dhvānta-dīpikā ॥ 181 ॥

Meaning

She who is known through intense spiritual practice, whose nature transcends the six pathways of manifestation, the embodiment of causeless compassion and the lamp that dispels the darkness of ignorance.

आबाल-गोप-विदिता सर्वानुल्लङ्घ्य-शासना ।
श्रीचक्रराज-निलया श्रीमत्-त्रिपुरसुन्दरी ॥ १८२॥
श्रीशिवा शिव-शक्त्यैक्य-रूपिणी ललिताम्बिका ।
एवं श्रीललिता देव्या नाम्नां साहस्रकं जगुः ॥

Pronunciation

ābāla-gopa-viditā sarvānullaṅghya-śāsanā ।
śrīcakrarāja-nilayā śrīmat-tripurasundarī ॥
182 ॥
śrīśivā śiva-śaktyaikya-rūpiṇī Lalitambikā ।
evaṃ śrīLalita devyā nāmnāṃ sāhasrakaṃ
jaguḥ ॥

Meaning

She who is known even to children and simple folk, whose command none can transgress, who abides in the royal Sricakra, the glorious Tripurasundari. She is Shiva, the embodiment of the unity of Shiva and Shakti, Lalita Ambika. These are the thousand names of Goddess Shri Lalita.

इति षष्ठः पटलः ॥

iti ṣaṣṭhaḥ paṭalaḥ ॥

This ends the Sixth Chapter, the Stotram Patala or Chapter of Litany, in the Lalita Tripura Sundari Shodashi Tantra.

Epilogue

This is everything, directly from the mouth of Bhairava, the form of God of Gods, Shiva and this is all us humans would ever know about Kali, and her Shakti. Most would never even come close to grasping the powers Shiva and Parvati bestowed upon humans, because it was meant to not be for everyone. If there were all kings in the universe, who would they rule over. Lalita Tripura Sundari Shodashi tantra, is a book of magic, literally, and if one truly with a devoted mind, practices the rituals dictated by Bhairava, there is not a lot of things that cannot be achieved. You could be wanting enlightenment, riches, respect, rule, liberation, anything and everything that you want to attain, you can get, but you the choice as to whether you actually want it, belong to you, because it is you who chooses to believe or not, it is you chooses to practice or not, and it is you who makes the choice whether to reap the results or not, for divinity always stays there, it is the worshippers who come and go.

www.ingramcontent.com/pod-product-compliance
Lightning Source LLC
LaVergne TN
LVHW050802061126
851857LV00012B/652
* 9 7 8 9 3 6 3 5 6 1 6 3 2 *